THE INSID[E]
THE BRE[XIT]

THE ART OF THE IMPOSSIBLE

HOW TO START A POLITICAL PARTY
(AND WHY YOU PROBABLY SHOULDN'T)

ANDREW REID WITH SIMON CARR

\B^b\
Biteback Publishing

First published in Great Britain in 2023 by
Biteback Publishing Ltd, London
Copyright © Andrew Reid and Simon Carr 2023

Andrew Reid and Simon Carr have asserted their rights under the Copyright, Designs and Patents Act 1988 to be identified as the authors of this work.

All rights reserved. No part of this publication may be reproduced, stored in a retrieval system or transmitted, in any form or by any means, without the publisher's prior permission in writing.

This book is sold subject to the condition that it shall not, by way of trade or otherwise, be lent, resold, hired out or otherwise circulated without the publisher's prior consent in any form of binding or cover other than that in which it is published and without a similar condition, including this condition, being imposed on the subsequent purchaser.

Every reasonable effort has been made to trace copyright holders of material reproduced in this book, but if any have been inadvertently overlooked the publisher would be glad to hear from them.

ISBN 978-1-78590-812-5

10 9 8 7 6 5 4 3 2 1

A CIP catalogue record for this book is available from the British Library.

Set in Adobe Caslon Pro and Futura

Printed and bound in Great Britain by
CPI Group (UK) Ltd, Croydon CR0 4YY

To our supporters and others across the political spectrum who worked so hard to bring about Brexit and have been so badly let down by the failure of Parliament to honour the view of the majority.

CONTENTS

Foreword *by Nigel Farage*	vii
Introduction	xiii

Chapter One	The Great Brexit Betrayal	1
Chapter Two	It's Always Later Than You Think	11
Chapter Three	Everything Is Harder Than It Should Be	19
Chapter Four	A Vertical Take-Off Party	37
Chapter Five	An Even Rougher Old Game	73
Chapter Six	Chaos in the Commons	103
Chapter Seven	The Spirit of Improvisation	115
Chapter Eight	Remainer Derangement Syndrome	135
Chapter Nine	A Difficult Decision	163
Chapter Ten	The Future of Political Start-Ups	203

Conclusion	211

FOREWORD

BY NIGEL FARAGE

Has a book like this ever been written about the formation of a political party? If there has, I haven't seen it. A wealth of evidence has been taken from the meticulous records that Andrew Reid kept during the Brexit Party's launch and its year-long existence. Emails, texts, messages, drafts, diary entries, board minutes, company resolutions, notes on scraps of paper – it's a treasure trove of communications between the principals of the party and will be of enormous interest to students, academics, the public at large and indeed anyone thinking the time is right for another new political party to be created.

Many people do think that. Sixty-one per cent of Britons

would like to see a completely new type of political party take on Labour and the Tories. 'Starting a political party' is even on the syllabus in some sixth forms. For better or worse, it's a growth industry.

The 250,000 words in Andrew's files are the closest thing to a contemporaneous record of a political party's history. This book is a distillation of that material and gives a rare – and very readable – insight into a political start-up. The way the party came about, the time we took to launch at the right moment, how internal problems were dealt with, the way relations were conducted with state agencies, suppliers, critics, opponents, supporters. The sheer scale of the difficulties we faced – starting a party, dealing with the legalities, launching it, selecting candidates, going into an election and coming out on top in a few months – will be a revelation to anyone who thinks politics is a rational, rules-based undertaking.

After twenty years with UKIP, I knew enough to realise that I couldn't be involved in the party machinery and lead the campaign as well. A political organisation takes two or three completely different sorts of brains, attitudes, mindsets. You can't canvass two media regions a day, do a public meeting in the evening *and* worry about the merchandising, or the invoicing, or the filing of papers at Companies House. And yet, as the book points out, without this attention to detail any political project will fail. A party machine is like an air force squadron's ground crew. Without engineers, mechanics and administrators, the pilots never get in the air. The project doesn't fly.

That's one of the most underappreciated things about politics: it's much more difficult than it looks, everything is happening at once and everyone has a different version of every event. No single person knows everything; no individual can do everything. There may be a plan, a road map, but events, dear boy, will conspire against you. The trick is to keep heading to your destination without getting distracted, dismantled or thrown off in the wrong direction.

Andrew's records keep us anchored in the reality of the time. The way our opponents ran interference on us is pretty entertaining (more looking back on it than at the time, I admit). The fake websites and billboards, the attempted stings, the campaign the Electoral Commission waged against us, the difficulties of getting a bank account and the banks' fear of 'reputational damage' are pretty shocking. And that's without the behaviour of the Tories.

But the support we got was incredible. It still amazes me. We had financial contributions from hundreds of thousands of British citizens and the votes of millions in what turned out to be a pivotal election in British political history. We had a fantastic team of people who brought it off, some at great personal cost. Some people lost their careers – the Establishment is still very Remain-minded and tends to spit out those who disagree. Some who fell in the field were brought down by enemy action, others by friendly fire. I really do share their pain because I ran into a brick wall at the end of it all myself. By the time of the general election, the Brexit forces we had brought into being were flowing along new channels: for all our success in a proportional election, in a first past the post system we could only split the vote and let in the enemy, as had happened in Peterborough earlier in the year.

The final test, maybe the greatest test, of our underlying principle was whether to put country before party. The decision to stand down half our field of candidates on the eve of an election was the hardest thing I've ever had to do in politics. An awful lot of people put their heart and soul into a campaign they were never allowed to complete. But voters wanted a resolution to the great conundrum of Brexit, and our full, national presence in the 2019 general election might have put that in jeopardy.

* * *

What we are left with now is the sense that the battle hasn't ended. At most, we've reached the end of the beginning. Very few of the benefits of Brexit have been realised. There's been precious little deregulation. The bureaucracy clings to European legislation like a security blanket. The Establishment elites are in thrall to a minority of intellectuals and academics who view Britain as uniquely wicked with a shameful past.

FOREWORD

Identity politics is causing irreparable damage to young people. And more important than anything is the government's commitment to Net Zero. It's as big as Brexit. It will limit the prospects of this country for fifty years if we don't get it right. If the government doesn't carry the people with it, all sorts of demons will be released.

But that's for the future. If we learn the lessons of this short, sharp, crisp little book, maybe we'll pull it off again.

INTRODUCTION

I am a firm believer in the people. If given the truth, they can be depended upon to meet any national crisis. The great point is to bring them the real facts. And beer.
ABRAHAM LINCOLN, MAINLY

It was December 2018.

The decision to leave the European Union had been taken two years earlier in a referendum in which 33.5 million voters took part. It had been the largest democratic exercise in the UK's history. It produced for Leave a narrow victory in percentage terms, but there were well over a million votes in it. Had it been a constituency-style vote, there could have been a 200-seat majority for Leave – bigger than Tony Blair's 1997 landslide. The people had been asked to speak and 17 million British voters had said, 'We vote to leave the European Union.'

Whether their verdict would translate into action was not at all clear. It wasn't paranoid to think that although the referendum had been won (or lost, depending on your viewpoint), the Establishment simply wouldn't let it happen.

A website for a Brexit Party had been registered but initially no one needed it and, as the world thought, no one ever would. The voting public had been reassured by their Prime Minister, Theresa May, repeatedly telling Parliament that 'no deal is better than a bad deal'. She was insisting that we were leaving the EU whether the negotiations succeeded or not. She had invoked Article 50 shortly after the referendum and as a result, the negotiating period began on 29 March 2017. Exit would take place two years later, on the same date in 2019 – neatly avoiding the UK participating in the European Parliament elections that happened every five years.

But, sadly, things had not gone well for Theresa May. Twenty points ahead in the polls, she felt confident in calling a general election. Faced by a dysfunctional Labour Party led by an extreme anti-British leftist, she wasn't alone in thinking she would emerge with a fifty, sixty, possibly eighty-seat majority to strengthen her negotiating hand. Even those who doubted her judgement came to think it was a shrewd move – right up to the opening salvos.

In what might have been the single worst campaign since Michael Foot's 1983 manifesto, the Prime Minister lost seats, her majority, her authority and threw Brexit into jeopardy.

Only by relying on the support of the Democratic Unionist Party was she governing at all. She had taken the British public for granted. She thought they had no one else to vote for. It was – it always is – a grievous error.

Now the oppositions she faced were many.

Parliament was against her. The Speaker was against her. The media were against her. The legal establishment was against her. The Supreme Court had ruled she lacked even the prerogative power to invoke Article 50 without primary legislation passed by Parliament. The Brussels negotiators were winning every round, every time, with every appearance of effortless superiority.

A proper Brexit was looking less and less likely.

Encouraged by the shambles, Michel Barnier, the polished Eurocrat acting for Brussels, saw a negotiating opportunity. He sensed weakness in the British position. Not one but two Brexit Secretaries had resigned. He must have felt that the civil service as well as the British Parliament was on his side rather than on the side of their own negotiators. He scented victory. He made an audacious play. He announced there would be no further negotiations, no more changes before the exit date.

Leading Brexit campaigner Nigel Farage's misgivings had been growing for a long time – in fact, since shortly after the referendum result. After the exhilaration of that win his immediate thought was, 'How are they going to mess this up?'

As early as the autumn of 2016 he wrote, 'The great Brexit betrayal has begun.'

For the next two years, his friends and supporters asked him, 'What are you going to do?' and, 'When are you going to do it?' To both questions he gave holding answers. He was waiting to declare his hand. Although he didn't know exactly what that hand might be.

Things were worsening at every step. Surely they couldn't get even worse? But, per the old political truism, 'If you think things can't get any worse, it's just a failure of the imagination.'

Theresa May's 2017 Florence speech tied us into European institutions in a transition period of an unspecified length. It also withdrew any threat of cutting off contributions to the EU budget. The following year there was the Chequers deal which tied us into the Customs Union with a common rule book. It was increasingly clear that Theresa May was working for a Brexit In Name Only.

Something else crystallised in the autumn and winter of 2018. It was a hunch Nigel had that grew into a certainty.

There was no way a settlement was going to be reached by the exit date in May of the following year; the positions were too far apart. Parliament was rejecting the Withdrawal Agreement – one side saying too much had been given away, the other side saying too little. There was no resolution possible in the time frame.

What did that mean?

INTRODUCTION

It was inconceivable that Barnier would allow a no-deal Brexit. They would have to extend the date of the exit. That meant the European Parliament elections on 23 May would come into play. That meant the UK would be sending new representatives to the European Parliament. *That* meant Brexit-minded representatives needed to be elected. The alternative – a strong showing by Remainer politicians – would be taken to mean the country had cooled on the whole Brexit project. It might mean Parliament voting for a second referendum. It could mean remaining in the Customs Union. That would mean the country would remain under the supervision of the European Court. That would leave the country subject to all the regulations of Brussels without any say in their making. A wounded EU Commission would be in a position to exact revenge on the country that had defied its authority, its very existence. Vengeance would be a high priority, to discourage any other country from attempting the same exit.

Therefore, Nigel Farage's logic led to an ineluctable conclusion: a party strongly committed to Brexit *had* to win the European elections.

That party wasn't UKIP. The party Nigel had left after the referendum had been taken over by its extremists and was retreating to the fringes. The Conservative Party was equivocal – half of their MPs and most of their peers were strongly Remain. The Lib Dems were pathologically Remain and no one quite knew where Labour stood. No, a proper

Brexit campaign meant creating an entirely new party, with a new name, a new organisation, a new unified membership structure and a new constitution. We had to campaign, man the polls and win a clear majority of seats – all in the space of twenty weeks.

So it was that one afternoon in January, when I was seeking winter sun, my phone rang beside the pool of a hotel in Palm Beach.

'Andrew?'

'Nigel!'

My wife rolled her eyes. I had promised her that after five years with UKIP I was out of politics for good. She knew what politics was like, and it was fair to say she had had enough of it. The endless texting, phone calls, dramas, crises, late-night meetings, ridiculous hours, the bubbling inferno that is high-pressure politics. The whole environment that Nigel had been living in day and night for twenty years. He seemed to thrive on it. And now he was on fire: 'Brussels, Andrew,' he said. 'We need to go back to Brussels.'

Why did he call me? Where did I fit in?

Some years ago, the author, entrepreneur and political mechanic Alistair McAlpine had called on me to help him with his defamation actions against the Speaker's wife, Sally Bercow, and others including the BBC and ITV.[*] He had been

---

[*] His case succeeded and we established a precedent that tweets had a separate legal status from a conversation around a kitchen table.

maligned by innuendoes linking him to a nasty conspiracy theory, including an on-screen blunder by Phillip Schofield while interviewing then-Prime Minister David Cameron. Having got to know him somewhat, I read his book *The Servant*. This consists of a series of lessons he learned in the service of Margaret Thatcher. Alistair was a grandee in his own right with a family fortune, a peerage and the aristocratic attitudes that went with these things – so it was striking that he characterised himself as a Servant to anyone, albeit with a capital S.

The purpose of a Servant, in his sense, is to serve a Prince – the person with the Idea, the Vision, the Purpose. The Servant predicts things that the Prince will need to smooth his path as far as possible, to ease hostile competitors out of the action, to raise funds. To make, in short, everything possible for the Prince to fulfil his great mission in life.

The Servant stays in the background as far as possible. He (or she) values anonymity. He has no ambition for himself. He organises, arranges, dispels, soothes as much as he can the environment around the Prince.

I realised I had been, over the years, a Servant to Nigel Farage.

A decade before, I'd made available a floor of my offices off Brook Street to give UKIP a London headquarters. When needed, and there being no obvious alternative, I served under the title that Nigel insisted I take, UKIP's National Treasurer (not to be confused with the Treasurer, who did the work of the Treasury). I served as an intermediary in the defections of Douglas Carswell and Mark Reckless from the Conservative Party (agreed, not the most glorious of successes). And having no ambitions myself, I was able, when necessary, to help check the rising ambitions of others (nothing is more destructive in politics than jealousy).

So, my role over the years evolved into a background intermediary between other people and Nigel – sometimes a gatekeeper, sometimes helping to fix things. There were occasions when things went awry – a wheel coming off, a big end giving way, a failure in the fuel supply. We shall be going into those in sometimes gruesome detail.

My background, incidentally, is that of a solicitor, a deputy High Court cost judge, an entrepreneur, a property developer, a farmer, and – perhaps the most unusual element in such a career – a professional racehorse trainer. In that last endeavour I trained 178 winners, including winners on Derby Day, Oaks Day and, in 2005, the All-Weather Derby. In all, this wide range of activities has put me in touch with people at all levels of the British social spectrum, from aristocrats and high financiers to some of the finest people I know – country people who work with animals.

In any event, Nigel's phone call set in train events that would lead to an unprecedented event in British political history.

INTRODUCTION

A start-up party would win twenty-nine seats in the European Parliament in its first election. For context, the Lib Dem Remainers won just over half that number. The Conservatives, the governing party, won four. It was a colossal victory for a party that hadn't existed just a few months before. After clinging to power by her fingertips for months, the Prime Minister finally conceded when faced with the inevitability of our win. The result allowed the country to emerge from the interminable, Kafkaesque negotiations with a clear road ahead to a successful, independent future.

How had it come to this?

CHAPTER ONE

THE GREAT BREXIT BETRAYAL

Nigel Farage walks in and it feels as if the sea has parted.
He holds his hands aloft as the faithful roar him on,
a messiah without portfolio.
THE GUARDIAN

Thus *The Guardian* described Nigel entering the autumn rallies of 2018. He was still a member of UKIP. He was also the vice-chairman of Leave Means Leave. But he was there on his own account, independent of any party or organisation.

So, what was he up to in the midst of this roaring crowd? Why was he calling 'the People's Army' back to the standard?

He had no sense that Brexit was going to happen in any meaningful way. As he understood it, the 'great Brexit betrayal' was well under way. What he was doing in front of this crowd was essentially research. He wasn't commissioning a marketing company to ask people to grade their concerns on a scale from one to ten. He was directly engaging with his supporters to discern the answer to crucial questions. He was testing the waters; he was gauging the public's attitude and appetite for further action on his great cause. He was after people not just from the left or right but across the political spectrum to tell him crucial things.

How much of his understanding was commonly shared? Did they feel as he did that the negotiations had gone badly? That Parliament was behaving disgracefully? That the forces of Remain were strong and strengthening? That Brexit itself was in jeopardy? That the referendum decision and wishes of the majority were of no concern to the Establishment? And was a new party needed to campaign for their goal?

The sense he was getting from his research was yes, yes, yes, yes, yes and… not yet. The failure of negotiations had cut through. The public was aware we had agreed to pay £39 billion to the EU as a parting gift before the negotiations had started. People had noticed that our chief negotiator had resigned and so had his successor. That Theresa May seemed to be playing a double game – that she was saying 'no deal is better than a bad deal' in public but was actively constructing a very bad deal indeed behind closed doors.

But the question of a new party to campaign for a proper

Brexit? All through September, October, November it was not yet, not yet, not yet.

Public patience with the Prime Minister had not completely run out.

Timing is everything in politics. What seems solid today may look ridiculous tomorrow. Are your people ready for what you want to reveal? Is there an identifiable rallying point? If you fired the starting gun, would you have runners ready to take off? If you go too early, you fire the gun and nothing happens. The movement collapses and will struggle to recover. These things can't be taught, but maybe they can be learned by bitter experience. They are felt, they are absorbed by rare individuals.

The crowds Nigel was drawing were certainly looking for something. 'Hope,' says Richard Tice, the founder of Leave Means Leave. 'They felt let down by the government. They felt everything going in the wrong direction. They felt helpless at the start of the meeting – by the end they were in a different state of mind. You could feel it. It was palpable.'

So, *The Guardian*'s 'parting seas' was a good description. That implacably Remain paper was one of the very few media outlets to pick up that something was happening. Nigel was energising crowds from Sunderland to Bournemouth. Audiences of 500, 1,000, 1,500, in Bolton, Birmingham, Torquay, Gateshead, Harrogate. He was connecting with people across class and regional boundaries in a way that only Boris Johnson could equal. He had promised an earthquake in 2014 and had caused one when UKIP swept the European elections. Now he was promising a revolution. A strange promise from a conservative-minded politician (and that won't be the last oddity or contradiction in this story).

But as much as public opinion was gathering momentum behind him, he was actually holding back.

* * *

The *Guardian*-reading public know Nigel Farage as an impulsive populist. He is very quick on the uptake and people like to say because he is quick that he can't be a strategic thinker. 'He can spot openings in a market and take snap decisions,' one of his colleagues was quoted by the BBC as saying. 'But he does not think strategically. He thinks and acts on the spur of the moment, as you would expect of a trader.'

It's a judgement that sounds true but isn't. You can tell from Nigel's career that he is a remarkably strategic politician. In 2002, he turned down the leadership of UKIP, feeling it was too early for him. Four years later, feeling ready, he took on the role and took it from a 2 per cent party to one that triumphed at the 2014 European Parliament elections. His success forced Cameron to promise the in/out referendum that changed British history. These things don't happen without a strategic sense behind them.

Add to this that he saw the 'Brexit betrayal' before anyone else. He saw immediately that the Withdrawal Agreement wasn't going to pass through Parliament. He understood the appeal of a second referendum to the public and how skilfully it was being orchestrated. That, incidentally, was the reason he didn't turn Leave Means Leave (with its 150,000 contacts and supporters) into a political party to fight the European elections. He saw that if there were a second referendum, they would need LML as a non-political organisation to apply for the official designation to lead the campaign.

That is strategic thinking.

The rallies were the beginning of a plan, as yet unformed. They were part of a process of discovery, to find out how to proceed. Direct engagement with electors and supporters was an exercise to feel how the public were connecting with Brexit and to sense whether it was enough.

Enough for what?

That was something he left a little vague. It might have been a campaign to fight a second referendum, for instance.

Whatever it was, they billed it as a We Are Ready tour. He told his crowds:

I didn't think we'd have to do this again. I thought we'd

won on June 23 2016 in what was the greatest democratic
exercise in the history of this nation ... I feel more fearful
than I've ever been ... that we're going to finish up being
sent back for a second referendum.

He talked about how the EU had forced countries into a second
referendum if they'd voted the wrong way once. He could feel a
real possibility that the same would happen with the UK.

My message is it would be wrong for us – much as I don't
want a second referendum – not to get ready. Not to prepare
for the worst-case scenario. We must not fail in our preparation.
We've now got to start forming branches and active
groups all over this country. We've got to be out there. ... I
don't trust our Prime Minister. I don't trust our politicians. I
think they will in the next few months betray us completely.
Let us be prepared for every situation. And if there is a second
referendum we will win it by a much. Bigger. Margin.

Applause. Exit. Foot-stamping, fist-pumping energy.

* * *

I have often wondered what it is that Nigel has. How does
he get his audiences going? All politicians want to be able to
do what he does but very few can. Other speakers might say

exactly what he says – in the same words and cadences – but the audience is left exactly where it was in the beginning. Nigel can be electrifying.

What is it? What's the combination that so few politicians have?

I've boiled it down to three or four things: the things that mark him out from the career politicians who have slid into public life along the well-worn paths taken by researchers, advisers and assistants – those who have depended on patrons, sponsors and lubricated relationships with influencers and party brokers. The back-roomers have never been judged on their ability to move public opinion, to address large public meetings, to hold their own on *Question Time*, to face that fast bowling on the 8.10 slot of the *Today* programme.

For me, these are the main qualities that make Nigel different.

1. He engages with all sorts of people from every walk of life without awkwardness or fear of disagreement. As he used to say on his phone-in programme, 'Ring me up and tell me I'm wrong.' In an age when party leaders orchestrate public situations so that they're surrounded by their own staffers and activists, in fear of a challenge – this makes him an exception.
2. His voice fills a hall. There isn't a better voice in British politics, with its gravelly edge and its full bass register. It

carries. All the breath turns to voice. It's a parade ground voice, with authority, a sense of command. It's not the careful, guarded voice that we in the office world tend to have. It seems to gather his whole personality and project it at his audience. When he's in public-speaking mode he has what the movie industry calls 'surround sound'. Together with the ease, the manner, the assurance he has – it's a powerful and very unusual combination.

3. There is also the fact that after twenty years in the European Parliament he understood Brexit at a visceral level. It was part of his character. The whole culture of Brexit vibrated in him. It's why he spoke best without notes, without reading his speech. He was the single person in British politics who represented Brexit – and the public understood that when they heard him speak about it. No one else is trusted on the issue. When he left UKIP, its membership collapsed. When the Brexit Party was announced, it didn't register with the media until he became leader.

4. He added what I believe to be the mystery ingredient for politicians. His audiences believed that if they followed him, supported him, voted for him – then things would actually change. Their support would count for something. He would realise the vision. He would make it happen. And this sense communicates itself. His supporters believed not just in the cause themselves – they believed *that others believed* Nigel would make the difference.

Hope and Change really are motivators, no matter how discredited the words have become. Barack Obama campaigned using those words, won a famous victory... and almost nothing changed as a result. 'How's that hopey-changey thing going for ya?' his critics put on bumper stickers. The President's battle cry was 'Dare to Hope!' His youthful believers thought their candidate was going to lead a spiritual revolution of world consciousness. Those who kept the faith were grievously disappointed.

Nigel wasn't promising anything nebulous or ridiculous. His mission was that one simple thing that people believed he could do: he was going to make Brexit happen.

When belief takes hold, it starts a chain reaction. His listeners were not just connecting with Nigel; they were connecting with each other. It's like wiring up batteries to each other – in series, they generate an ever-increasing charge.

So, while it may be possible to believe that the data specialists won the referendum, with the apparent discovery of 3 million non-voters – no one can prove it one way or the other. Personally, I believe that those 3 million non-voters would never have got to the polls without Nigel. Algorithms and memes and social media messages are all very well, but without a leader, a voice, a galvanising presence that people believe in, nothing happens.

The Brexit movement that started in the 1990s had been travelling through a generation like a deep-sea swell. Now that we were approaching shore it was rearing and breaking. Without ever losing its forward momentum, that tumbling mass of personalities, passions, experiences and convictions had somehow to be formed into a coherent, disciplined, regulation-compliant body.

Organisation is the essence of politics: without a party machine behind them, leaders have nothing to lead.

CHAPTER TWO

IT'S ALWAYS LATER THAN YOU THINK

Politics is one of the most heavily regulated industries in the UK. The challenges around a new party are many, various and great. We had little more than four weeks from the date we were registered to the launch of the party. And from there, we had only six weeks to the election.

These are impossibly short timescales for what we had to do.

Every serious party must be able to apply expertise to deal with a host of disparate matters: financial donation systems, data protection, privacy law, employment law, safeguarding, electoral registration, computer systems, property leases, insurance, legal actions, frauds, impersonators and angry supporters. And that's before we even start thinking about selecting candidates or standing for election, let alone winning seats.

Parties need a leader, but they also need infrastructure. They need an administrative machine. They need a big back office. A lot of this work is unglamorous, grinding, exhausting. It's opening mail sacks and sorting letters into piles. It's filling out deposit slips and taking cheques to the bank. It's itemising the requirements of hundreds of different authorities all over the UK and making sure their different deadlines, timings, demands are met. It's getting cash out of the bank and walking it through the streets, forwarding purchase orders, responding to supporters, answering queries that have been raised a hundred times already.

It is also extremely high-pressure. Mistakes will be seized upon by the regulatory bodies and then the media. Late filing, late registration, absent invoices, confused paperwork, the wrong signature on a document – these can cause very serious problems. And because it's politics, everything is under-resourced and happening fast, in a rolling ruck with all its drama, teamwork, rough play and professional fouls.

At a very basic level, at the beginning of 2019 no one outside Nigel's innermost circle of two or three was absolutely sure which way he was going to move. There were any number of organisations and individuals committed to his cause, any one of which he might join.

Leave. Vote Leave. Leave Means Leave. BeLeave. Better Off Out. Get Britain Out. Change Britain. Campaign for an Independent Britain. Conservatives for Britain. Labour Leave. Economists for Free Trade. European Research Group. Grassroots Out. Veterans for Britain.

And of course, there was UKIP.

That benighted party had fallen under new management and was reversing every hard-fought improvement Nigel had made over a decade. In his only similarity to Tony Blair (bear with me), Nigel had created an electorally successful party, led it for a decade and when he left, the fringes took over and set a course back to irrelevance.

If Nigel had wanted to take back UKIP, could he have? He had certainly done so before, more than once. In one sense, it might have been easier to join an existing entity than to start a new one. Such an organisation would have had administrative systems already in place, a bank account arranged, everything squared with the Electoral Commission.

But what a bloodbath of sacking and purging there would have had to have been. The drain on energy, finance and political credibility would have been immense. Nor was there that most precious quality in politics: time.

And, most importantly, we knew that the Brexit Party had to appeal across the political spectrum. We had to be a broad church in a way that UKIP could never be.

As for other, less conspicuous, parties, many of whom were calling for Nigel to join them – could their culture withstand the shock of the Farage way of doing things? Would their values, when put to the test, hold? Were they fearless? Were they actually prepared to endure social ostracism? It takes a special kind of person to live with the contempt of erstwhile friends and relations. And those hostilities were very real. We came across many, many cases of our supporters losing their livelihoods when their loyalties came to the public eye. Brexit was not for the faint-hearted. Our opponents were not just merciless but inventive in their mercilessness. They didn't just throw milkshakes, they shut down meetings, picketed our venues, chained themselves to chairs, harassed families, hounded people out of jobs, attacked businesses with fake reviews, scared off customers, organised boycotts. Even we, the battle-hardened, were taken by surprise at the reception outside our launch rally. No – Brexit wasn't for those who had something to lose.

So, there were many reasons why we needed a new vehicle. Nigel had been talking with a UKIP colleague, Catherine Blaiklock, and had encouraged her to get on with registering a party called the Brexit Party. He believed that had he tried to register it himself, the Electoral Commission would have blocked him. 'Alarm bells would have gone off all over the Establishment.' He wanted the party sneaked onto the political scene: 'I wanted to be the horse that comes up on the rails.'

Catherine had been involved in Nigel's UKIP as its economics spokesperson. An intelligent high-flyer with a trading background running an options desk in the City, she had been an energetic proponent of Brexit for years – but had never voted in any election before 2015. Her reasons for getting involved were interesting. It wasn't that the Leave vote had radicalised her or shown her that politics could give a voice to the previously unheard – it was the reaction of the Establishment.

She'd been at a dinner at Christ Church, Oxford (where she'd been a scholar – no mean feat, coming out of the care system in the 1980s). It was just after the referendum result and her old tutor spoke after dinner. Her first words were a shout from her inner core: 'I'm SO ANGRY!' Which is how Catherine realised the battle for Brexit had only just begun.

'I didn't know these feelings existed,' she said.

> The wailing! And then the abuse! I had Leave friends who were bankers, or lawyers, or in finance, and they all wanted out for any number of reasons – the way Greece had been treated, or the way they tried to bounce us into the euro, or the crazy legislation that had come out of Brussels. Nothing like the motives that Remain said we had.

Catherine formed and registered a company at Companies House called The Brexit Party Ltd in November 2018. She then applied for registration with the Electoral Commission on 8 January 2019. I helped her get through the molasses of the Electoral Commission's procedures (which got ever thicker the further from their preferred political views we went). By the first week in February it had come through. The Brexit Party was granted permission to stand candidates in British elections.

That was no small achievement. Suddenly there was a Brexit party, it had a name, a constitution. It existed.

The constitution filed was, in our first setback, quite unfit for purpose. Most importantly, it provided for our having *members*, and that directly contradicted the novel idea underlying this endeavour. We were to be the first British political party that didn't have members. We'd have a handful of directors and everyone else would be supporters.

It was a brilliant decision and how it came about is a little mysterious. Several of us believed the idea was our own, but we must all defer to Nigel, who says it was the one idea he took from Geert Wilders in the Netherlands.

While accepting that all good ideas are the property of the leader, I maintain, discreetly, that it had also occurred to me. My particular motivation stemmed from the fact that I had been the poor fellow in UKIP dealing with its more eccentric members, its fringier members, and, alas, with the occasional nutter. The hours I have spent dealing with the repercussions of men dressed in Union flags giving Nazi salutes – that is time I will never recover. It occurred to me that if we had supporters rather than members, we wouldn't be in danger of being tarnished by such people claiming to represent us.

Furthermore, Nigel and I had concluded that the most destructive element of UKIP had been its governing committee, its NEC, riven with conflicting ambitions and rivalries. That model of governance meant the leader always had to deal with internal opposition and spent endless time and energy negotiating the factional interests. That was a democratic conundrum that needed a solution.

In any event, we registered with the Electoral Commission but the party didn't register with the public. We didn't break through into newsrooms because the Brexit Party was nothing without its leader in waiting. Without Catherine, there wouldn't have been the registration, the beginning. But without Nigel, there was no Brexit Party.

Nigel – the master of timing – had been holding back from fully committing to coming in as leader. I think he was waiting to see whether we could produce a functioning party structure. Nonetheless, the pause was useful. Then, in our first series of crises, it turned out to be essential.

All through January there was business to conclude. There was much preliminary work to be done before anything could happen. We needed a bank account. We needed a website. We needed a way of taking donations. We needed an accounting system.

But these are all normal business functions. How hard could it be?

None of us knew the answer to that.

None of us had ever done this thing before, conjuring up a party out of nothing in the blink of an eye. In fact, no one had ever done it in the sort of timescale we were facing – there was no one we could consult. The simple fact is that starting a party is entirely different from running an existing party.

One fundamental source of confusion is this: no single person knows everything about the endeavour. There are many different aspects to a party and no individual can understand them all. We are the proverbial blind men describing an elephant.

For those who haven't come across the ancient wisdom, it concerns five blind men encountering an elephant for the first time. One blind man walks into the animal's side and declares, 'An elephant is like a wall.' Another who has grasped the tail says, 'No – an elephant is like a rope.' And so forth. The parable tells us that all our knowledge is partial. And very often wrong.

So, with politics, data people are inclined to say it's about algorithms. Social media directors say it's about memes. Some strategists say it's about percentages; for others it's issues or policies to deal with issues; others can show by algebra the direction to take. Optimists say it's about hope; pessimists, about fear. Even the leader who has the culture of the party vibrating in him – even he doesn't know everything. Not what jokes are unfolding in the social media division, or what invoices are unpaid in the finance office, or who is doing what to whom in Hartlepool.

From that vantage point at the beginning of the New Year, 2019, we all underestimated what was involved and overestimated the time we had to do it in.

CHAPTER THREE

EVERYTHING IS HARDER THAN IT SHOULD BE

What does a start-up party need?

First things first: a political party needs an office. People need somewhere to sit. A party isn't something you want to run from home – the incoming traffic is continuous and destructive of private life. You need proper offices with, ideally, some level of security – keypad entry for one thing. If you are attempting something controversial, you will attract demonstrators. They may be armed with paint cans, loudhailers, and milkshakes to throw at you. This is not a family-friendly business.

But basic realities are very basic. You need room for your filing cabinets, desks, computers. Coat stands for your staff. Tea- and coffee-making facilities. Water stations. A system for processing stationery. All the small details of office life.

Open-plan is all very well, but you must have spaces where you will not be overheard. You need a meeting room, preferably with a soundproof door – there will be voices raised. Oh, yes, voices will be raised.

If you aim to have a wide reach, you need a central base to reach out from. If you aspire to be a national party, you need to be in the centre of national life, which – for better or worse – is London. If you can beg, borrow or pay for central London, so much the better. I'd been able to provide an office suite in my building for UKIP headquarters some years before. Nigel found that to be a key moment in that party's professionalisation. If your HQ is in the leafy suburbs or in Bournemouth, or Cheltenham, or Sheffield, it will send out a signal of how you see yourselves, of what you are. If your address is a Post Office box, you are saying publicly that you have no backers, that there is little courage behind your convictions and that you may be gone tomorrow.

There are a number of general points that may be usefully noted before we start:

- As soon as you have an office you will have office politics. And there seems to be an interesting rule – the further away from power you are, the more intense the struggles.
- Never underestimate the ability of your staff, colleagues and co-workers to have opinions contrary to the party's best interests.

- Remember that politicians are often unwilling to answer a question with the words 'I don't know'. Bear this in mind if asking for technical or legal advice.
- The person with their fingers on the keyboard, be they never so low in the hierarchy, can have more influence over what is written than you, as their manager, might imagine or indeed wish for. Be careful who has control of the keyboard.
- A wide range of personality types will be needed in your endeavours. There are many different functions to be fulfilled. Some are detail-oriented, others are process-oriented, some intuitive, some inspirational. Some positive, some negative. The variety is essential. Some qualities may seem difficult, or trying, or exhausting to be with, but negative qualities may conceal important virtues. Someone who knows that the rules have to be obeyed may be known as intransigent or pernickety. But this insistence on obeying tiresome regulations will be what keeps everyone out of jail. Therefore, tolerance of the idiosyncrasies of others is essential. Many people's politics can be summarised as: '*If only everyone could be more like me!*' This attitude will hinder, not help in, your endeavours.
- There is an immense difference between creating an organisation and running one. The two systems require two very different sorts of people and mindsets. Start-up people have to be able to improvise, to get out of trouble, to be prepared to leap with only a cursory look. The unexpected

will always happen, and things can always get worse. Once the organisation is established, things change. At that point you need people who attend carefully to administration in such a way that they don't need to improvise their way out of difficulties – the difficulties don't occur in the same way.
- A good general rule was coined by Lesley Katon, our head of candidates. It might be called The Circumference Rule. She said, 'I never took notice of the fun and games outside my own area. Candidates were my job: that's what I cared about and all I concentrated on.' The rule suggests that the more an individual recognises their circumference and the more they stay inside it, the better for everyone.

* * *

In those early, chilly days of January Catherine took an office, paid for with her own money, in Victoria Street. This was officially head office. There was at the same time a parallel office in Brexit Street, or Great Smith Street as it appears on the map. It had at different times been the home of UKIP, then of Leave.EU under Arron Banks and Leave Means Leave under Richard Tice. Throughout, Nigel had held the middle floor with his long-term team around him. As a result, the three floors enjoyed a smoking terrace. It suited the organisation to have two sets of offices – the Victoria Street one went on record as head office. There, we had the media scrums, the demonstrators and, once, a visit from the

Metropolitan Police, whose investigations were stymied at the front desk. At the other address, the bulk of the campaigning, outward-facing work was done.

I sat outside both of them, in my own offices behind Brook Street. I remained at a distance, such that I was in touch with but not inside either theatre of operations.

Now for the sake of discretion and convenience, Catherine had put her own name on the registration forms as leader. She was officially not just the leader but also the owner of the company that held the party. She was its sole shareholder. This became significant, as events unfolded.

The quorum of staff in a party is, according to the Electoral Commission:

1. Leader
2. Treasurer
3. Nominating officer (to submit election candidates' papers and gain approval for the party's logos and descriptors)

One person can in theory fulfil all three roles, but if she (or he) does, there must be another officer registered. A political party only comes into existence when two or three are gathered together.*

---

* Be careful, you who wish to start a new party: your outriders and supporter groups operating under different names can complicate your life if they are deemed by the Electoral Commission to be political parties in their own right.

For treasurer, I suggested Catherine ask an old associate to come in – a chartered accountant with extensive political experience and knowledge of the Electoral Commission, Mick McGough. Treasurer is, apart from the leader, the most important role in any political party. You may wish it were not so, but money is the blood in a party's veins. The flow must never get blocked and by the same token it mustn't be haemorrhaging. Either is always possible when there are different parts of the operation growing almost spontaneously.

The strategy department will want money for polling, events want money for the country-wide meetings, the messaging people want money for branding, trademarking and logo design. Finance always need more resources to check donations and process purchase orders. The head of this and the director of that will always find that more of something is needed and feel empowered to commission it or buy it in on sixty days' credit. That has to be brought under control. And bear in mind, everyone is working twelve-hour days and nobody quite knows what the proper way of doing things is. All this needs systematising into a purchase-order system (something that will irritate all levels of the organisation).

More important even than this, the treasurer must have a grasp of the ever-changing rules invented and imposed by the political regulator, the Electoral Commission.

Mick was a safe pair of hands. He had been in UKIP for ten years and for many of them had been a branch chair.

Mick had stood for Westminster three times, is treasurer of the Orphan Fund at the Chartered Institute of Journalists and was well-known on the embassy circuit. He had a standing invitation to the Irish embassy in the legendary days of Ambassador Bobby McDonagh. Most impressively for some, he is treasurer of the UK branch of the Kentucky Colonels.

Catherine asked a contact of hers from Norfolk to come in as nominating officer – the other necessary appointment.[*] So, they were three. She also realised that comms were going to be important and on Nigel's advice she asked the veteran Brexit intelligence of Gawain Towler to come in as a consultant for four hours a week. There were more than four hours a week in it. When he presented his first bill, he suggested he go onto a monthly retainer.

And where was Nigel in all this? Through January and February, he was making supportive noises and occasional media reports emerged that he was taking the Brexit Party seriously as a vehicle, but he wasn't stepping in to front it, to project it, to establish it in the public mind. Even towards the end of January he told the *Sun on Sunday*:

There is huge demand for a party that's got real clarity on this issue. You can see and hear the frustration welling up

---

[*] Tracy Knowles, whose ability was much admired. Capable, smart, concise (a rare and valuable asset in politics), she was a great help in the early days. Sadly, we lost her services later on and she didn't get the reward she deserved: neither she nor I was able to get her nominated for the seat she wanted.

out there ... If the government goes back on its word and betrays the millions of people who voted for Brexit then we need a party prepared to stand up and fight for it. I'm fully prepared for Article 50 to be extended or revoked and if that happens, I will re-enter the fray.

Note those two instances of *if* and the subsequent *I will*. He was continuing his public policy of wait-and-see, of biding his time, of building expectations. And he was wise to do so, for things could go any one of a number of ways. Theresa May's Withdrawal Agreement might get through Parliament, for instance. However unlikely, it was conceivable we would leave the EU on 29 March. Anything was possible at this stage.

The *Financial Times* was promoting a story that EU lawyers took the view that even if we overran the deadline British candidates still wouldn't be eligible to stand for election to the European Parliament. It was possible that the European Court of Justice would pull a fast judgment banning us from the election. Maybe the European Commission would issue a directive. Maybe the Electoral Commission would step in.

Other eddies in the stream were getting stronger all through the beginning of 2019. A petition to revoke Article 50 had by that time received over 4 million signatures (they said that was a lot; we said it was a little). The clamour was growing ever-louder for something called a 'People's Vote' (as if the referendum hadn't been that). And perhaps most significant of all, Speaker Bercow had given the first indication of his plan to empower and project the forces of Remain in Parliament.

Such were the uncertainties, the variables that contested with each other, producing different possible outcomes in different analyses.

As for me? I sat where I was most comfortable – in the background. Part of my function in the early days was to try to keep the infant organisation in some sort of balance when we ran into difficulties. I hope I was to be relied on to provide impartial opinion, to settle arguments equably, to warn, to advise quietly.

That wasn't always easy in those early weeks. With Nigel half-in and half-above the fray, we were somewhat in limbo. He was waiting to make sure we were capable of putting the basics of a party together. 'You can't be the front man, the creator of the content, the salesman *and* be in charge of the administration of the party,' he said.

Nevertheless, until we had got to the point of having a functioning party administration, it wasn't at all clear who was in charge. And when there isn't clear authority in a party, confusion will prosper.

Catherine was the nominal leader and she had to make progress. She was taking people on and performing executive functions. Around her, many others – advisers, volunteers, consultants, fundraisers, strategists, experts of various sorts

– were circling. All had opinions. All had advice. All wanted budgets for their vital functions. Many would be happy for a position. There was confusion. How was it all to be managed? Who would carry the can when things went wrong?

* * *

Among all these decisions requiring experience and guile to negotiate there were the simplest tasks to complete, tasks that have been made ever more complex over time.

Opening a bank account, for instance, the most basic of business operations, is no longer a straightforward matter. Even a blameless company making grommets and widgets will find it takes significantly longer than it did a generation ago to open an account. The bank wants to be assured that you aren't using their services for purposes of terrorism, that you aren't career criminals and that (shockingly to my mind) you don't represent a reputational risk. For a political party like ours, that was a determining factor. Banks fear to be tainted by association in any way, shape or form with controversial politics (which, for some reason, means anything to the right of *The Guardian*).

So, bank officers look through the attacks, irregularities and general excitements that attend any political party and they take a view on what the association will do to their brand. They consult their risk register. They cower in expectation of receiving a number of campaign letters from our opponents expressing 'puzzlement' or 'disappointment' that the bank is providing services for a 'racist hate organisation'. They are invited to consider how they would like their premises sprayed with silage that has been dyed the colour of blood. Peace-loving protesters have a new range of media-friendly techniques at their disposal to increase love and harmony in the world.

These considerations make a financial institution cautious. They make it hesitate.

So, to that extent, bullying tactics are successful. The left has done a remarkable job in the last decade or two in changing the culture of a country. Now, they will be pleased to know, it is increasingly difficult for organisations to practise their right to operate. No doubt we will come to their aid when the pendulum has swung away from them and banks start cancelling their accounts.

For us, a bank account had become urgent because money was piling up in Catherine's PayPal account. Even before we launched, supporters were pouring money in beyond any expectation. It needed to be housed in a conventional bank account.

Our excitement was not shared by the institutions we approached. The process of discovery between us and two high street banks began by being trying, then exhausting and finally insulting. The company structure, they wanted to know all about that. For a bank to want to scrutinise our constitution seemed unusual. Then they wanted confirmation of the shareholding of the company. Then they wanted a letter on a solicitor's letterhead affirming that the share register was an accurate account of the shareholding. And then, presumably mistrusting my signature on my company letterhead, they demanded to see the register itself. Who held the trust document? Could the bank handle donations from UK nationals living in the US and contributing in dollars? It wasn't just young officials wanting boxes ticked all down their forms. We didn't understand at that point that the banks were running scared of the reputational risk of being associated with our political project.

In the end, Richard Tice – now the chairman of the party – opened up a channel with his bankers. They provided a temporary account for us and the funds flowed in. What a performance it was to get that simple administrative function completed.

But it didn't end there.

Later that year, Richard Tice had transferred the party's account to the high street bank Metro. The handover was taking an unconscionable amount of time, so Nigel got their chairman to have a word with their compliance department – the ones who were conducting their exhaustive due diligence. 'It'll be done in a couple of weeks,' it was promised. Two months later the compliance department were still at it, interviewing anyone who had the authority in the company to make deposits, let alone withdrawals (and Mehrtash A'zami, our third treasurer, was in the process of increasing the treasury staff). They eventually opened the account, and we went on equably enough for over a year until they sprang an entirely novel procedure on us: they gave us sixty days' notice of closing the account. No reason was given. There was no suggestion of impropriety. 'I'd been a director of a hundred companies,' Richard Tice says, 'dozens of banks, hundreds of accounts. *Never once* have I had a bank treat a customer like this.'

Tice wrote to Andrew Bailey suggesting that the Bank of England offer a 'bank account of last resort'. Democracy was ill-served if popular parties had no access to banking.

This all reinforced the feeling that we were operating outside the boundaries of respectable society.

* * *

Who? Whom?
Vladimir Ilyich Lenin

In those first weeks, there was a fundamental question to be settled: who makes the decisions? Whose word counts, whose writ runs? Nigel was our leader *in absentia*. Who was to make the decisions? How were we to gather opinion to weigh the options? How were we to avoid the quicksand of a representative NEC?

All established parties have a process to allow opinion to be expressed and policy to be made (almost always without letting it override the leadership).

A membership party will have a process something like this:

You, as – say – a Labour Party member, have a policy idea in front of your fire in Derbyshire. You want to incentivise the use of sustainable light bulbs. You work it up with the whys, wherefores, pros and cons and...

1. You put it to the chair of your branch committee.
2. The branch chair then submits it to the constituency general committee. If approved there...
3. They send it to party headquarters. If they like it, they'll put it into a policy commission.
4. An annual National Policy Forum inserts your idea into a document (assuming they approve it) and it goes to the...
5. Annual conference to be considered by the Conference Arrangements Committee, which gets elected just as the conference begins.
6. If your faction wins places on the CAC, your idea will probably be approved and then presented to conference attendees to be voted on. If it gets a large majority, it then becomes policy (which may or may not be binding on the leadership, depending on your party constitution).
7. It may or may not find its way into the election manifesto (on balance, probably not).

Seven levels of approval for your brilliant idea to reduce VAT on eco-friendly light bulbs.

The Brexit Party couldn't make decisions like this.

We knew all about local organisations from UKIP – branch meetings, constituency committees and their reports, recommendations, resolutions. The European Parliament elections, if they took place, were scheduled for 23 May. We had a little under three months before the campaign proper began – ten weeks to establish our infrastructure and get enough administration in to process donations, to deal with the Electoral Commission and the Information Commissioner, to select candidates, to get the message out on social media, to build a machine to get the vote out.

The normal rules of democratic politics could not apply. So, here was the first decision in front of us. How do you structure a party that is to be led by Nigel?

We weren't going to have a mass membership OMOV (one member, one vote) party. We weren't going to have branches and a show of hands for policy. We were going to be a party funded by our supporters, but they would have no formal say about our policies or proposals and they would never be direct representatives of the party's position on anything.

That was a bold idea.

But then what of the governance of the party? Who was responsible for its stance, its behaviour, its candidates? Its spending, its funding? If that was all to be the leader's responsibility, who was going to control the leader? Was the leader susceptible to control? It was Nigel, after all.

Nonetheless, the first school of thought was:

1. We must have a strong administrative team to contain and focus Nigel's political energies, his gifts of projection and persuasion, and to force him into essential message discipline and talking daily to donors to raise vital money.

The alternative lay at the other end of the spectrum:

2. Make Nigel an unassailable leader. Make the party a company with him as the majority shareholder. Give him, as it were, a block vote to override any opposition.

The arguments in favour of (1) were persuasive and practical. The supporters of a strong administrative team made their powerful points, saying: 'The fundamental need of a party is money. Without money we can't advertise, we can't organise, we can't leaflet or set up regional operations. Nigel is brilliant, but he won't talk to donors in a disciplined way every day unless he's made to.' This view incorporated another popular point: 'Nigel needs message discipline. This shooting from the hip gets us into all sorts of trouble.' And: 'He really needs to cut down on the blokey booze 'n' fags thing. It puts the professional, AB types off. We've got the CDEs; we need the upper demographics. It's a no-brainer.'

So, considering everything carefully and taking it all in the round, we went with (2).

I knew from experience in UKIP how time-consuming political decision-making is even when half a dozen officials are involved. How much listening is involved. How much arguing, persuading, cajoling. Because an interesting feature of all politics at all times is this: when people know a decision can be contested, they will organise support for their own position. Factions form. All parties are troubled with factions – loose and shifting allegiances, affections, resentments. It's human nature. It's politics. You can't stop factions forming, but there is always a balance between too little input and too much.

Without sharp, central decision-making, we'd never make the deadline. We were in a unique, time-limited situation. Giving Nigel control meant that decisions would be – or could be – made promptly. Giving him sole authority put the responsibility on his shoulders alone. It had been his 25-year campaign, and if we were going to pull it off, this was to be the Year of Nigel Farage.

There is a temptation in the back office of any political party to think that officials and directors and trustees know better than the frontline politicians. Should we be going so heavily on immigration? Don't we need more broad-spectrum policies? Why don't we have more voter ID information in our key marginals? Are we in danger of peaking too early? Isn't this too aggressive? Won't rebutting that slur just give it more prominence – we'd surely be better to keep our heads down?*

Maybe they're right, maybe they're not. The view from the sidelines is never the same as that on the pitch. Having played this game at the highest level for twenty-five years, Nigel was – whether right or wrong on any particular decision – the moving spirit of the campaign. He embodied it. It inhabited him. The whole culture of Brexit vibrated in him. In my view his instincts were the ones to rely on. And bear in mind that politics happens so quickly that instincts are very often more important than researched, considered responses hammered out by committees.

So this democratic party, this party formed to further the course of democracy, began with Nigel as a boss unfettered by any possibility of internal competition. Not even the chair of the Chinese Communist Party was so secure in his position. Such are the curiosities of politics.

---

* A political party also needs people who are less interested in policy and more interested in the physical dimensions of a mass-mailing leaflet sent by the Post Office. One small party stood a candidate in Glasgow and failed to present their leaflet in the right format; the Post Office refused to deliver it. These small disasters are all part of the larger comedy.

CHAPTER FOUR

A VERTICAL TAKE-OFF PARTY

Difficulties accumulate and produce a friction which nobody can imagine who has not seen the inside of a Brexit Party start-up.

CARL VON CLAUSEWITZ, MAINLY

We started a little tentatively in the New Year and launched the party three months later on 12 April, six weeks before European Parliament election polling day.

What had we accomplished in the first two months of 2019? We were halfway through our journey to the start of the election campaign. What had we achieved?

Much more and much less than I'd thought.

I see in one day's emails during those very early days the chaotic range of matters that were (or weren't) being dealt with. The constitution, for instance, had been queried by the

Electoral Commission. Catherine wrote me an email with a subject heading:

'This constitution is rubbish.'

A strong point, well made. The constitution isn't just a formality. All sorts of plays have been made through the rule book in various parties at various times – nomination deadlines, quorums for meetings, voting rights of members, how to depose the leader. It's not a dusty document; it can be mobilised. There were certain aberrations and inconsistencies in the document submitted to the Electoral Commission.

Catherine forwarded their comments pointing out that we had led them to believe our intention was to have only a central party without members or branches, only supporters. But then the constitution had allowed for the creation of a branch structure and Catherine asked, reasonably, who other than supporters would run them?

That had to be addressed. Which of us was capable of drafting constitutional amendments? This was one of many, many questions that faced us.

On the day's agenda were the following:

- A vexatious request from a pseudo-supporter who had registered with us in order to gum up our works with litigious requests for information.
- Who was in charge of data protection? The new people being proposed were more expensive than the previous

people who had been appointed. Remind me, why did we change our minds? Should we change it back?
- Have we applied for new identifiers with the Electoral Commission? Could someone be commissioned to deal with the Electoral Commission? Who would commission them?
- Candidates – are we sure it is a reasonable idea to charge them £100 each to cover the cost of their vetting? Might that look like we are profiteering?
- Where are we on the re-registering of the party away from a for-profit?
- Is this person a good candidate? Apparently not – I thought she was ex-UKIP. We need to be extremely careful not to become UKIP 2.0.
- How are we going to agree on a logo design and colours? Who owns the logo we're using? Has copyright been assigned?
- Paid registered supporters paying £25 each – was that within GDPR (data protection) guidelines? Were we allowed to take the money if we didn't give them something extra, like a premium membership or a T-shirt?
- We were trying to migrate Leave means Leave supporters onto our Brexit Party database legally. Where are we on that?

One day's list of decisions and action points!

Oh, and we shouldn't forget the utterly insignificant point: who was drafting the disclaimer at the end of emails – the one that said, 'If you aren't the intended recipient of this email…'?

Someone has to write that, or edit it, or cut it down. The standard one is too long, too obtrusive. If you use the standard version of things – like the terms and conditions – you become an object of mockery, with your opponents saying you've taken your text from a Chinese takeaway in Norwich.

In all the hurly-burly we had had one stunning success. And by stunning, I mean so stunning that there isn't really a word for it. Through January we'd got some of the preliminaries in place and one afternoon in early February, Nigel's media and digital adviser – not a website builder of great experience – put together a website and put it online. It called for support. On the same day, the *Financial Times* quoted Nigel as saying the Brexit Party was 'a live vehicle'.

With no promotion, no social media, no advertising and no marketing presence our expectations were modest.

On Monday morning, I answered a call from Nigel's inner office. They were ringing to report on the performance of the website over the weekend. We'd gone live at 4 p.m. on Friday. In the previous sixty hours we'd had 35,000 registrations.

I assumed I'd misheard. 'What is that, *hits*, are they called?'

'Registrations. They are supporters who've registered and paid £25 a head each.'

'And you're saying *35,000* supporters have registered?'

'For £25 a head.'

'*Over the weekend?*'

A VERTICAL TAKE-OFF PARTY

We had hoped for support, but this was beyond any expectation.

At the office, I was shown the financial screen and saw supporters piling in. *Ting! Ting! Ting!* Every *ting!* was £20, £25, £30 – sometimes £100. They came every thirty seconds – but sometimes there were bursts when the *tings!* came so fast they merged into each other like a drummer playing a high-hat. Every contribution I saw was an individual pledging support in the most sincere way: with their own money. Funds were coming in at the rate of £2,000 to £3,000 an hour.

Nor did it stop. It didn't even slow. Every day more and more. By the end of the week we had 100,000 registrations. One hundred thousand people in a week. None of us had seen anything like it. In seven days we were pushing Conservative Party numbers in terms of registered supporters.

The Brexit Party was a vertical take-off party.

'I have to say,' Nigel remarked later, 'that holding back for six months was the hardest thing I'd had to do in politics – and it bore the greatest results. We took off like a rocket.'

Two streams of consequences flowed from that beginning. The first was benign. Substantial backers had been holding off until they could see that we could exist without them. When they saw the scale of support, they turned to their chequebooks.

The second stream was malign. The Electoral Commission couldn't believe we were generating such support from so many people. Even when we showed them the screen where they saw for themselves the cascade of contributions, they wouldn't have it. They had no explanation for the scale of popular support and for the modest quantum of each contribution. Eventually they explained it to themselves as 'bots'. It must be Russian 'financial bots' making so many contributions. And so began the Commission's long and ultimately unsuccessful campaign to discredit our funding.

Nigel was more involved now. I remember particularly the important matter of our slogan, our positioning statement, the call to action. As Nigel put it:

> I was in favour of anything that said, 'Give Them a Kicking' or 'Teach Them a Lesson'… quite a negative approach, in retrospect. Our polling genius Chris Bruni-Lowe and the newcomer Christopher Harborne came out of a huddle and had a different idea. The first time they told me, I didn't agree. They didn't let it go. The second time they came back with it, they persuaded me. They said Brexit was part of a much bigger problem – that while people weren't connected with the political machinery anymore, they really wanted connection. Brexit in that sense had radicalised them.

So, the slogan they were proposing was Change Politics For Good. Nigel said he took a long time to come round to it but as soon as we adopted it, the whole character of the campaign changed. 'It became positive,' he said. 'It was all based on the good of the country. The whole aspect of what a sceptic was changed in those four words.'

* * *

All through February, party matters multiplied.

I had no contact with the process of selecting candidates, messaging or starting the business of campaigning. There were any amount of other matters taking up our time. Small, petty, trivial details that could trip us up on the finish line if they weren't seen to properly.

A friendly character in UKIP let us know that their team had selected their candidates, that they were ready to go into a campaign. We didn't even have a list of applicants to select candidates from. As Catherine pointed out, things that parties took a year or several years over we were planning to do in weeks.

We were in no state to fight an election.

We would launch the party on 12 April – and bear in mind the election, if it happened, would also require campaigning to start in April. And yet, as late as March, I received this from Catherine: 'As things currently stand, there is no structure to the day to day running of the company, so organising or delivering anything is difficult and inefficient. The GDPR task exemplifies this. Which staff do we train? Who will have day to day responsibility?'

On 3 March, I wrote: 'You are all working without a roadmap. I will speak to Nigel as he needs to nail down his route to success, otherwise we are all over the place.'

There was no decision-making process. But that could only start when the decision makers were in place. The fact that we were at all ready to campaign when the deadline fell – that was a testament to a British spirit of improvisation.

The head of the Channel Tunnel project once said that the French were much more methodical than the British in their planning. They got into trouble less than we did – but when they did get into trouble, they found it much more difficult to get out. They got trapped in their plan. Without the pragmatic British spirit, the Brexit Party would have taken two years to be ready for the elections.

* * *

Thanks to Richard Tice, we had two bank accounts opened and ready to go. Our PayPal processes had been established and all security processes completed (it had taken nearly a week to get money out of that system).

We had all documents filed at Companies House, the Electoral Commission and the Information Commissioner's Office. The new constitution had been amended and presented. The logo was done. The website was up and the thank-you email was going out automatically.

We'd drawn up our non-disclosure agreements to be signed by people entering into the organisation to work on sensitive systems or procedures. An auditor had to be appointed and indemnity insurance arranged.

Note that these work streams are all without any political effect. They are purely administrative, technical – and apparently endless. The paperwork was prodigious. The toing and froing a bureaucratic odyssey.

Catherine had been working on a delivery plan and identified the two organising elements that anyone starting a new party would want to consider.

There is the corporate side, with its administrative functions, and what she termed the 'product' side, which dealt with the party's message and the management of the team that will 'sell' it. You have to have both.

She therefore suggested the following centres of responsibility. We needed a chief executive to oversee the entire organisation. And under that person, an office to ensure electoral compliance.

We needed officers who took responsibility for:

a) Ensuring that the party and its people do not transgress electoral and regulatory obligations.
b) Devising internal guidelines and setting the party's rules of engagement with third parties.
c) The filing of all official electoral returns and accounts.

Then, she suggested, we needed an office of policy development to define the mission, the brand and the party's manifesto.

It was a description of a professional organisation that had the great luxury of time to put things together. Just putting a manifesto together was, from experience, a major undertaking.

We solved the manifesto problem by not having one. Everything we wanted and were working for could be put on a credit card-sized pledge card: We're going to leave the European Union.

We solved the conundrum of guidelines and obligations by assigning those duties to the essential officials – treasurer, nominating officer – and by keeping the administration so tight we didn't need more. For other functions, we looked to old colleagues.

There had to be a press office handling the media. We had the veteran Gawain Towler. Within that, we needed people handling social media. And we needed money to be raised. There George Cottrell, a part of Nigel's close personal office, came into his own. 'Nigel doesn't like asking for money,' he says, 'and Richard Tice is so rich people think he should be giving rather than asking. So, it fell to me.' George was instrumental in bringing in the country's largest political donor (more of which later). And then, the website that Dan Jukes pulled together in an afternoon also played its part.

We needed people to be speaking with authority, secure

and confident in their positions. And they needed to be proven, loyal and trustworthy.

The downside of a pop-up, cross-party team is that the ties that bind you are political and ideological rather than personal. People who have served in the trenches together have a bond that goes beyond reason or belief.

We had a matter of weeks to put all this together.

It was a formidable programme of work. I won't pretend it proceeded with Teutonic efficiency. In fact, I dare say there is a popular sitcom to be written about a new political party.

Time is the great enemy. Everything is under that inexorable pressure.

We had to select seventy-odd candidates to represent us in the election. We had to vet every one of them. We had to rank them in order – and that is a process that would stretch the patience and managerial talent of almost anyone. 'But I thought *I* was getting that seat!' And, 'Why aren't I higher on the list?' And a universal, if unacknowledged, sentiment, 'Why are *they* so high on the list?'

Catherine was very disciplined, perhaps as a result of her banking experience and her familiarity with organisational tables, and she suggested a practical way of proceeding, along these lines:

a) Setting the campaign messages and establishing the 'grid'
b) Producing official campaign materials

c) Planning and organising the physical campaign – travel, venue booking and advance teams
d) Managing media appearances (TV, radio, live debates etc.), including preparation and obligatory rehearsals
e) Brand policing of candidates' speeches, appearances, remarks and conduct
f) Electoral expense accounting and official returns

Unfortunately, her sensible, practical plan met reality in the same way acids meet bases.

Every political start-up will encounter the same thing. People come together to effect a great change and the closer they come to each other, the more they disagree on what to do and how to do it.

Catherine was dealing with a multitude of issues coming at her from every direction. Each problem generated a number of advisers either all saying one thing or a variety of conflicting things. If you ask a question of politicians, only the rarest will say 'I don't know' if they don't know the answer. (Nigel happens to be one of those.) She also noted correctly that there was no forward planning. Everything was coming together in a way that can be kindly described as 'organic'.

As she noted, 'Now we are faced with future chaos – all hell will break loose next week if there are going to be elections.'

We were within sight of the start of the campaign. It was emerging above the horizon. The visible deadline concentrated minds, but I'm not sure whether it increased productivity in the organisation.

I should say that these matters are intensely personal and it's no part of this book to chronicle the ins, outs, ups and downs of who said and did what to whom and why they did or didn't do what they should have done. Yes, there were falling outs, conflicts, misinterpretations, misunderstandings. Voices were raised. Veins bulged. People were hurt, sometimes badly. Politics is, as people say, 'a rough old game'.

Mind you, if it seems rough in the Brexit movement you should see how bad it is in the anti-hate parties.

* * *

An unacknowledged truth about the practice of politics is how difficult it is. Practically everyone outside the arena despises politicians. The public brands them, above all else, as idiots. But the public have no real idea of what it's like – the range of decisions that have to be made, the ever-present uncertainties, the hostile environment created by the media and your opponents, the speed at which things happen. There's also something perverse in the political mindset, something destructive. Richard Tice said when asked about the difference between business and politics: 'In business, you pull a lever and things happen. In politics, people try to destroy the lever.'

It's true I thought at times that UKIP had been infiltrated by MI5 and saboteurs were in place to destroy the party. It was Robert Conquest's Second Law: the best way to predict the behaviour of an organisation is to assume it is being run by a secret cabal of its enemies.

The reality is that politics demands an extraordinary mix of qualities in its practitioners. To succeed, even to survive, a person needs convictions but suppleness. Patience but urgency. An appetite for personal news from everyone in the environment – but discretion and the ability to keep one's counsel. In all their relations, office-holders need to gauge the level at which other people are operating – one of half a dozen levels – in order to respond appropriately. They need to know what they don't know. They need to be able to balance priorities, to know which battles are worth fighting, to know when to forgive and when not to.

Very few of us have this mix of qualities. But that's not the half of what's required.

Leading politicians need astonishing physical energy. They need to be able to face criticism, anger, loathing, without letting these things deform them. They need all the qualities of Kipling's 'If —' along with a certain deadliness of purpose, something that is only released in special circumstances. As I say, politics is harder than its critics understand, and their misunderstandings are vigorously expressed.

Any fair reading of Nigel's political career must construe

A VERTICAL TAKE-OFF PARTY

it as the result of his conviction that Britain did not naturally belong in a political union with a continental bureaucratic apparatus. Add to that, he travelled many years in the political wilderness ridiculed and isolated. His steadfastness in pursuit of his goal is a most remarkable political fact.

Had he wanted money, there were many other avenues open to him, far more profitable. People of his ability in the long boom years made multiple millions in the City. Did he pursue fame? He pursued Brexit, and fame came along with that, eventually. What politician shuns the limelight?

People who think politicians are idiots would be shaken to find out how bad they would be at it themselves. Journalists are probably worse than anyone – they make *ex cathedra* assertions which are overturned by events, and no one confronts them with their mistake, miscalculation or misspeaking years later, as if they had committed a moral faux pas, the way they do with politicians.

The fact is, politics is facing and dealing with fast-paced events every day and every hour – every one of which may have consequences far beyond their initial significance.

Try this as a taster. A very small example. It's one of the myriad of problems and questions we were confronted with in those first weeks while waiting for essential services to be established.

The name. What should we have done about the name? What would you have done?

The registered name was The Brexit Party. A name is one of the most important things for a new party. The Brexit Party said what we were about and what we wanted to do. It was not only a name; it was a statement of intent.

But always with a name, you can rely on the fact that no one agrees it's a good name until the decision's been made and everyone moves on. There was a wide range of opinions, all powerfully expressed. It was said by some to be too narrow. It was a single-issue name. It needed to evoke a larger vision of society in order to include the wider aspirations of a freedom-loving electorate.

Or, others said, it needed a call to action in it. It needed a sense of purpose. It needed motion, motive, it needed an appeal to all sections of society – an appeal we could leave vague. What about… Alternatives for Britain?[*]

Yet others pointed out that we wanted to plug ourselves into the common-sense values of the great, silent majority out there beyond the metropolitan elite and their fashionable concerns. Why not the Country Party?

A marketing view was that politics is like selling canned goods or telecoms services. Why not follow the lead of the most successful launch in recent times and call it Orange. Or because it's small-c conservative, Blue. The Blue Party.

No, said another. It's going to be perceived as a one-man

---

[*] As long as you don't mind the association with the right-wing party Alternative for Germany (bearing in mind the term 'right wing' in Germany carries with it unfortunate associations).

party – why not make a virtue of that and call it The Nigel Farage Party?

The final word was left to the leader. Nigel said: 'Brexit is what we're here for. It's what we're going to do. Everything we want is summed up in three words. We are The Brexit Party.'

As it turned out, The Brexit Party was the wrong name. It didn't conform to what Gawain Towler calls the Aardvark Principle.

A party with 'The' as its first word appears towards the bottom of an alphabetised ballot paper. A party beginning with 'B' for Brexit appears at or near the top. European election ballot papers are ordered by the name of the party, not (as in British parliamentary elections) by the name of the candidate. But did it really matter?

The judge in the 1987 High Court case *O'Reilly v Minister for the Environment* in Ireland ruled that the evidence 'proves conclusively that, in Dáil Éireann elections over a period of nearly forty years, there has been a significant over-representation of candidates whose surnames begin with letters at the commencement of the alphabet'. He went on to observe that it wasn't so much a defect in the system as a 'want of care or a want of interest by the electorate'.

It seems to be important, if you have the choice, that your party be called something that puts you at the top of the ballot paper, not the bottom. What do you do about that? Was it worth expending energy to change it?

When we realised the problem at the beginning of March, we thought it was. We decided to go to the Electoral Commission to change the name. It wouldn't be difficult, surely. 'Kindly adjust the record to change The Brexit Party to Brexit Party. We enclose a cheque for £25. Thank you.' But our first treasurer, Mick McGough, was told by the Commission that there had been a deadline of 4 February to apply for such a change. They expected to take up to mid-March to effect such a change but it could be longer: the regulations allowed the Commission forty working days to complete the task.

Forty working days – eight weeks in real time – would take us perilously close to the start of the campaign for the European elections.

Did we still want to change the name?

What were the risks? Before the forty days were up, we would need to have printed all our election material. If we had a different name on the leaflets, the party might be declared invalid. Relations with the Commission were, so to speak, uneven at this stage. We couldn't risk relying on their goodwill. At the extreme, it was conceivable that by the time the ballot papers were being printed our name would still not have been finalised, thus putting at risk our entire presence in the voting booths.

Mick was emailing the Commission frequently but not receiving information he could rely on. The Commission were obliged to respond to Freedom of Information requests within twenty working days, he noted, but were unable to discharge one of their core duties – like registering a change of name – within forty-two days. He was incandescent when he discovered that the Commission had obliged The Independent Group for Change (Anna Soubry, Chuka Umunna et al.) by registering their name change within sixteen working days. When the Brexit Party name was changed to Reform, it took over two months.

Why this disparity?

One conclusion became our private conviction. We felt they were not neutral umpires. We were convinced by their actions that they were a profoundly Remain-supporting organisation. We found that their behaviour was consistently biased against the Brexit Party.

To my mind, the Electoral Commission is clearly not impartial, has attempted to impose duties on us beyond the governing legislation, has granted favours to those who fit with their politics and can be obstructive and vengeful towards those whose views differ. The facts – *our* facts – show it is not fit for purpose. As we came to find through the course of 2019, they were a manifest affront to democracy and had we had the time and energy after all the dust had settled, we would have pursued them in the courts.

This conclusion sounds wild; there's ample evidence for it in the following pages.

So, for a name, we were left with The Brexit Party. How many votes did it cost us? We can never know. Nevertheless, there were supporters out there emailing us in block capitals, accusing us of being idiots for not changing the name, and not registering every website address that sounded like the Brexit Party.

However long that discussion and decision took, it turned out not to matter very much – unlike our first major, slow-motion drama that so nearly turned into a crisis.

* * *

Catherine had set up the Brexit Party as a limited liability company. The question she came to ask was: is this the right structure? It looked as though we were setting up to profit from our great mission. It was a good point. She had formed the company in a hurry, and by herself, in something of a vacuum. So, we agreed to change our designation to a not-for-profit.

That doesn't sound like much of a problem. In fact, my legal colleague Christine Minty eventually solved it in her incisive way by advising us to write a new fifty-word addition to the articles of association. That was all we needed to do, in the end. Ah, but not until we had fought our way through a series – a saga – of legal advice and semi-professional interventions.

The first message sounded innocent enough.

In response to her request for a way forward, Catherine received a message from Lawyer #1 saying:

> This is a company limited by shares. I would have made it a company limited by guarantee. Attached is UKIP's articles, yours should be as close to this as possible. That being said, I am not sure it matters at the moment. You can change them very easily as the sole shareholder and director.

'You can change them very easily' became a haunting phrase.

He also felt the power was too centralised in Catherine. As we have seen, she was unique in British politics in owning a political party. She was not only the designated leader; she also was the sole shareholder in the company. It was an odd state of affairs: even in January, February, March – even after leaving the stage – she was the single shareholder. Lawyer #1 went on to say: 'If you place those shares you own in trust for the benefit of the party, that would accomplish the same goal (of spreading the power out away from a single person owning the party).'

We needed a quick solution to solve the for-profit stance we were in. There was a time pressure on the process – it had to be completed before Catherine could send the company documents to the bank in order to open an account and release the funds that had already accumulated.

But not so fast. Nothing is simple. Don't let time pressure rush you into error. The authorities are unforgiving.

So which company should we present to the bank – the original creation or the not-for-profit? How much detail would the bank ask for? And how would we deal with the Electoral Commission? They were touchy, strict on detail. Would they just flip the new details onto the existing registration? A Commission official had advised us in writing that it wasn't a matter for them; it was a matter for us. But could we rely on that advice?

It's not a question most political entrepreneurs want to be bothered with. It is a typically unrewarding problem, the solution to which will produce no credit to anyone involved.

Catherine had been canvassing opinion among experienced businesspeople who assured her there was no problem about the company number. 'No problem, no problem, everyone is saying there is no problem with the number,' she wrote to me. She wasn't happy with that.

One problem with the male domination of politics – I think it is a particularly male problem – is the need to appear omniscient. The need to be authoritative. The need to provide an answer with the sort of conviction that excludes any other answer. It doesn't always end well.

Catherine felt there was something missing in the reaction to her probing, something she couldn't put her finger on. Rather than acquiesce, she kept questioning those around her and not quite getting what she felt was in there somewhere.

I agreed with her and suggested she go back to the Electoral Commission for clarification. She asked them twice:

A VERTICAL TAKE-OFF PARTY

Are you confirming that I can change the company number and send you a new constitution which is exactly the same as the original but has a different company number?

Is the company number a unique part of the application process for the party or not?

One of the Commission's officers replied again, referring her to his earlier answer: 'It is not a matter for us if you wish to change your company number.'

There was something slightly 'off' about that as well. Looking back over it, the Commission may have been laying an exquisite trap for us.

I continued to agree with Catherine. 'No problem, no problem' was a dangerous assertion to take all the way in a political situation. It may even be a rule: there is never 'no problem' in politics. Administrators will be wise always to walk around a problem and view it from every side.

The common-sense view was that the company number could be changed by entering it on the registration form. There was another side to it. I wrote with my misgivings in order to support her:

A company is a legal entity and it is identified by its company number. What has been registered with the electoral commission is the company identified by that number. I

> do not think that changing the company number would be valid for the purposes of the Electoral Commission because any different number must relate to a different company (i.e. a different legal entity). There would be no point requiring registration if one legal entity could be substituted for another simply by allowing a change of number.

Re-reading this, I can see it is the sort of intervention that would drive politicians a little mad. It's like a tiny protruding nail that rips off the trousers of a man in a hurry. It's the undone shoelace that trips up a champion on the final stretch.

Catherine then sent me the advice of Lawyer #2. Remember, all we were trying to do was change the category of a company which hadn't at that point started trading. His advice took us a decisive step into a legal and commercial thicket.

He said:

Turns out that going from limited by shares to limited by guarantee cannot be done by ordinary filings at Companies House. The steps are:

1) Form a new limited company by guarantee (any old name not in use)
2) Change the name of the old company (again, anything you like)

3) Change the name of the new company to the now freed up name of the old company
4) Dissolve the old company

There is a slight risk in that the steps need to be completed successfully in short order. We wouldn't want to fall into any cracks that might open up.

Was it that complicated? Really?

Catherine sought a third legal opinion in the hope of establishing legal clarity. It arrived with words that chill the heart of any client. He said, 'Please sit down.'

His fine legal brain had told him in capital letters, 'It is NOT possible to keep the same legal personality by converting a company limited by shares to a company limited by guarantee.'

And being solution-oriented, he went on with a suggestion that many readers may wish to pass over:

It may be worth setting up a subsidiary of the Brexit Party that is The Brexit Party limited by guarantee ('the LBG') but I am not sure how you can transfer the ElCom registration.

Technically, the LBG is an entirely new company and the ElCom relates to your existing company, but the party might be able to act via a subsidiary if ElCom is happy with such an arrangement.

The above is so fundamental that I think you need to have decided on a plan to sort it out before tidying up the articles regarding limiting the role of members. Certainly, you need to come to conclusions about this before you start accepting money.

But there was a terrible possibility at the bottom of the email: 'I understand that the deadline for ElCom applications was something like 4 February, so if you have to make a new application you may be too late for elections in May this year.'

Missing the deadline was unthinkable.

These laborious legal details are only included to show how wretched things can get from first causes. We had begun with a simple company registration and in two steps we had been caught in a cat's cradle of complications.

Christine Minty had a view on this as well, and with a familiar example brought clarity to the proposed switch. She referred us to the practice of forming a new company and transferring assets (but not debts) into it. She said the whole point of that exercise was to prevent creditors of the old company pursuing the new company *because they were not the same entity*.

It is a matter for the Electoral Commission whether or not they would accept this, but I would not expect them to. In the old days one could simply do a transfer to a company and register it. Now both the transfer and the Companies House application form must give the company number so that Companies House can be sure that the entity subsequently transferring it is the same entity and not just the same name.

In summary: imagine we put in an application for our new not-for-profit version but with a different company number. It was possible that very close to the election, the Electoral Commission could rule our application as invalid. Our company name and number did not, in fact, match. That our name would not appear on the ballot paper. That the Brexit Party, with all its supporters, representing the largest share of the electorate, would be ruled out of the election on the basis of its different company number.

There were two further areas of intrigue in the proposed switchover. The existing company had 100,000 names of supporters in its database at that point. Could those names be legally migrated across to the new not-for-profit company with the different number? What would the Information Commissioner's Office have to say about that?

Many different priorities, advantages, disadvantages had to be balanced against each other in this simple exercise. As the company number was an integral part of the application to the Electoral Commission – as it was the unique identifier – it was what the Commission would rely on. If we wanted to go down that route of changing to a different sort of company, we would need a dozen documents of minutes, transfers and trust deed variations to be constructed, checked, double-checked, authorised, signed and sent off to Companies House before presenting the new entity to the Electoral Commission. We would then be relying on the Electoral Commission's goodwill to re-register us in under forty-two days.

This was something that should have been simple. That might have been executed by a director's PA in a couple of hours. On the other hand, in some extreme circumstance it might have done for us all; it might have taken the party off the ballot paper. There might have been no Brexit box to tick.

Catherine wrote to me:

> I suddenly saw it. What you had been saying. This is a massive political risk, not an admin risk. Goodness – just imagine Dominic Grieve or Soros looking into it. Either one of them could take ElCom to a judicial review the day before the election and have us disqualified. All we had to rely on was one junior boffin aged 30 at ElCom and a scrappy email.

Her initial misgivings were well-founded, her instincts excellent. The whole project might have been destroyed by that one company number. The Electoral Commission could have queried, delayed, shifted us past a deadline and left us off the ballot paper. If that sounds fanciful, please look at the saga of the sub-£500 donations and gauge whether they were impartial administrators of our democracy.

A VERTICAL TAKE-OFF PARTY

* * *

Catherine's view by early March was that she was coming to the end of the administrative horror – and in a sense it was true. Because we took a hammer blow from our friends at *The Guardian*. And then another one.

The left, as a generalisation, know better than the right how to conduct the great orchestra of the media. They have finely developed instincts as to what is sayable or not. They know how to whip up a panic. They understand how to end the careers of their opponents. They are accomplished because they love their work (essentially, hating anyone to their right). An organisation called HOPE not hate had for years been monitoring the social media accounts of people to the right of them on the political spectrum (or, as they call them, 'fascists'). They screenshot anything they might be able to use if those people ever came to prominence.*

It turned out that Catherine had retweeted comments from people such as Tommy Robinson, the angry, street-brawling activist, as well as from a prominent BNP member who had referred to 'white genocide'. There were also disparaging comments about Islam in her own name. Catherine had

---

* A word in favour of Matthew McGregor, the campaigns director of HOPE not hate. After the European Parliament elections had taken place, he was quoted as saying, 'The Brexit Party is not a fascist or far-right party ... Saying otherwise at this stage would not only be factually incorrect but would undermine our case against them.' It was a very decent attempt to raise the level of discourse.

deleted that Twitter account, but HOPE not hate had the screenshots. They passed the images on to *The Guardian*.

Nigel understood more than anyone the need to keep out of these particular controversies. They were no part of his political strategy or belief. As he wrote to her later, 'Whilst the assault on free expression and free speech in this country is a serious problem, it is not and should not be the territory of the Brexit Party. We would become a 2 per cent party.'

There was no question of Catherine Blaiklock being a racist. She wrote to me, 'I am the least racist person you could meet.' And I believed her. However, unfortunately it fell to me to put it to Catherine that she had to resign, and, as a trooper, she recognised there was no other way. The European election campaign was coming up on the horizon, no more than a month away. Had she stayed in place, the media would have focused on her deleted tweets to the exclusion of all else. It would have been a colossal distraction.

The lesson here is that if you want a political career, get off social media. It lives for ever. Whether you end up deleting your accounts or not, screenshots will be taken and stored.*

So it was that Catherine, the accredited leader of – indeed, the legal owner of – the Brexit Party, resigned. She put out a statement: 'My appointment as leader of the Brexit Party was only ever supposed to be temporary. My role working

---

* I am well-positioned to make this statement, given this was the outcome of the McAlpine defamation case – still the lead case on this issue.

with Nigel Farage was to set the party up and get it registered with the Electoral Commission, all of which has now been achieved.' There followed what she described as the 'Soviet-style confession', which was, and probably still is, mandatory.

Yes, it is a rough old game.

In terms of party administration, this was just the beginning. Catherine's resignation and her tormented feelings created a situation that required lawyers to resolve – and that is rarely ideal (I speak as a lawyer).

The way the company had been set up was complex and created many difficulties. If you came to it without prior knowledge, you would have thought it a game of Find the Lady – that sleight-of-hand operation played by street tricksters. We've seen how difficult it was to change the company into a not-for-profit; the subsequent transactions were in a different league.

Without going into detail, here were the broad outlines of the situation.

The Brexit Party had by this point been incorporated as a company limited by guarantee. Directors of the company had to be shareholders, shareholders had to be party members (who were different from party supporters) and shareholders' shares had to be transferred before anyone became a member and thereafter a director in order to exercise executive authority. Going the other way, if a director resigned as a shareholder, his or her share had to be deposited in a trust before being reallocated. If the shareholder was a trustee as well as a director, he or she couldn't resign – two trustees were required to be in position at all times, so a third trustee had to be appointed before the first could resign.

All of these processes took time, with forms submitted to Companies House and the Electoral Commission. At the time there were, in fact, only two members who were shareholders and therefore directors, neither of whom was Nigel, who was the Brexit Party in the mind of the public. Getting him into his natural place had to be in accordance with a new constitution that had been drawn up, then withdrawn and was in the process of being amended and registered with the Electoral Commission.

None of this was because 'politicians are idiots'. It was the result of errors forced by the speed of play.

The technicalities and processes of that situation were less important than the fact that Catherine felt rejected by and alienated from the party. Nigel wrote to her acknowledging that.

There is a lesson in here concerning the perils of operating at speed, under pressure, in a volatile atmosphere in which everyone wants to come out without any blame. There were extensive emails from all sides with misunderstandings, misremembered dates, misapprehended facts, accusations, counter-accusations. There was £200,000 of supporters' donations in a PayPal account which we couldn't get to, and that added extra spice to the arrangements. As long as the PayPal account was in this state of no man's land we were missing out on donations at our meetings – around £30,000 to £40,000 had gone uncollected.

And precision was paramount. A word misplaced in the documents would render them invalid. For instance, the mention of 'future profits' spoiled a whole day's work – the party being a not-for-profit in its amended articles of association, there were no profits to be had.

Would Catherine play ball all the way to the end? I had come to know her and to trust her. I believed she would. But it was pointed out that as sole owner and sole shareholder she had the power, if she chose to wield it, to appoint a new treasurer and convenor and have a majority on the board to do with as she pleased. Not for a minute did I think she would do such a thing. But it can't have been easy for her. I learned later that she was taking legal advice, and her adviser was proposing exactly this course of action. More than that, UKIP was offering an inducement to her to put the knife into Nigel and the Brexit Party and be rewarded with the top place in UKIP's MEP list. To her enduring credit, she rejected that out of hand, and all other similar suggestions.

At our end, we all had a sense of being caught in some fiendish web of technology. PayPal is extremely difficult to deal with in terms of transferring ownership. Or even getting them to do something unusual. As Catherine wrote to me, 'Yes, I can log in, but it will not allow me to do anything.' She gave Mick the login details and he penetrated the account far enough to change the password. But then it rejected his ID details and refused to let him do anything else.

The frustrations were considerable at the time. We were in the midst of one of the great constitutional struggles of modern politics and we couldn't get past the error message on our payment processor.

Few of my generation are particularly confident with these internet arrangements. Even Catherine struggled with turning off something called an auto-renew button on her 'dashboard' in her 'settings'. Phil Basey – the company secretary at the time – was fairly sure, he said, that it was to do with DNS codes, but that was several steps more than I could follow and was the limit of his expertise. He resolved it with the website developers, to whom this is ABC.

Even at the end of the process of resolving the company structure, with everything agreed, an element of comedy crept in. Nigel witnessed his own signature in the deed of retirement, which then had to be redone. Instructions had to be sent to the bank on party letterhead – which we didn't have. The expenses repaid to Catherine had to be sent by cheque (an electronic transfer would need money-laundering clearances), but we didn't have a chequebook and when we asked the bank for one they said it would take five days to organise.

At every step, it seemed, trivial lapses in procedure or process held us up or sent us back to the beginning.

There followed several days of pushing and pulling, with offers made and withdrawn on both sides until eventually we found ourselves, we thought, in clear and open water with only the election to worry about.

And then it happened all over again.

* * *

My good friend and long-time colleague Mick McGough, the party treasurer, came under fire. He too had made a series of social media comments that couldn't be justified. His concerned the Miliband brothers and their father Ralph – that they had 'shallow roots' in this country. *The Guardian* pointed out that Jews having little or no attachment to their adopted country is an 'antisemitic trope' and the Board of Deputies agreed. Mick still vigorously defends his remarks and describes himself as a long-time friend of Israel. Nonetheless, the realities of politics trump everything and there was enough in his comments to require action. It had been tough for Catherine and it was tough for Mick, but there it was: it fell to me to present him with the fact that he had to resign. 'I took one for the party,' he said. He resigned as treasurer, handed in his shareholding and took a step back. It was done, dusted and dealt with in twenty-four hours.

But we had lost our two most senior executives in two weeks. Our opponents must have been delighted. It had been a slick, well-conducted operation by their lights. They could continue their fiction that our party was the hateful embodiment of prejudice. We saw ourselves as the quiet majority saw us, as the reasonable voice of 17 million British voters, coming together to reinforce the biggest democratic vote this country had ever seen. And yet two of our foremost executives and directors had been decapitated before we'd even started.

The lesson, if there is a lesson, is to be careful with social media. I say that as someone who avoids social media altogether. I use an old-fashioned BlackBerry – one that doesn't have apps. Should I say 'have apps' or 'host apps'? I've no idea. Nonetheless, I will text. I have email. I've heard of WhatsApp, and I can see that it might have advantages, but it comes perilously close to social media for my taste. I am happy in my dinosaur status.

CHAPTER FIVE

AN EVEN ROUGHER OLD GAME

Politics is war without bloodshed.
MAO ZEDONG

There's no time to grieve for fallen comrades with an election in view. Phil Basey stepped up to fill Mick's functions as treasurer (among other roles that he took on).

He played a crucial role at a crucial time and it sent his blood pressure up to 220. He was our second treasurer and the only one among us who really understood the new GDPR. So, he came to be the man we looked to for compliance issues as well. He described his position later: 'There are two roles that guarantee anyone to be the first and second most unpopular person in the organisation, and I had both of them.'

He was the one saying, 'Where's the purchase order for

this? Who ordered this? I didn't authorise it.' And, 'No, we're not spending up to the allocation because we need a reserve for unforeseen spending.' He was invariably right. If we'd breached spending limits, the Electoral Commission would have come down on us very hard indeed. It takes substance to stand up to persuasive, powerful personalities who are driving things towards an epic conclusion.

For instance, now that it was clear we wouldn't need Leave Means Leave as a non-political vehicle to campaign in a second referendum, we could use their mailing list to campaign in the European elections. There were 150,000 names in their database – a significant boost to our campaigning power. We wanted those names. Nigel wanted those names and couldn't understand why Phil wouldn't agree to migrating the names over. The fact was that GDPR prohibited it.

Nigel was saying, 'These bureaucrats are telling me what I can and can't do with names who've willingly, voluntarily provided them? Is that what you're saying? It makes no sense.'

No, Phil said, the GDPR prohibits data collected for one purpose to be used for another.

'It's the same purpose!' Nigel said, more loudly than necessary. 'They all believe in exactly the same thing as the Brexit Party!'

Nigel, as a solution-oriented person, wouldn't let it go. 'Come on, Phil! We need those names! What's the solution? *There must be a solution!*'

Phil understood the existential consequences of flouting the GDPR. He replied, 'There is a solution, Nigel. The solution is *to comply with the regulation.*'

It takes substance to stand up to Nigel when the spirit is in him. Phil wouldn't budge. We ended up arranging for every name in the Leave Means Leave database to be contacted by email and over the course of a week or two (punctuated by Nigel's '*we don't have a week or two!*') 80 per cent of them replied consenting to have their data used for this new purpose.

Phil was also the one who refused our regional organisers access to the list of members. This caused considerable anguish. How could our organisers organise if they didn't know who wanted to be organised? The election was weeks away. The regional organisers asked the perennial question asked by political organisers in all ages: *how can we operate under these conditions?*

Phil's unpopular position came from an assessment of our far-flung battle lines. Were all our officials GDPR compliant? Did they all know what GDPR compliance was? Was every one of them guaranteed not to leave a data stick on a train? Was it absolutely certain that one of them wouldn't send the list of members to an unauthorised person, or press the wrong button and 'reply all' or publish the list on Facebook? Any one of these infringements would leave us open to fines from the Information Commissioner and possibly civil suits from the aggrieved.

And what about spending limits? We had more than enough money to spend up to the limit, but Phil refused to authorise it. He insisted a cushion of some £300,000 be left to cover for mistakes.*

Phil was the necessary opposite of Nigel. A party is a great endeavour, but start-ups must have people who can cope with the day-to-day details.

The things Phil was dealing with were the things that madden those with political ambitions. Those who are setting out to achieve impossible things – to get us out of, or get us into, the European Union, or create a socialist paradise, or abolish all quangos, or restore common sense to public discourse – are focused on the great destination. But these visions are apt to collapse when reality intrudes. Reality in the form of a question such as – has the relevant form been signed and sent to Companies House within twenty-eight days? If we give away a T-shirt with every supporter subscription, does that mean we have to register for VAT? If we don't give away a T-shirt with every supporter subscription, does that mean the Information Commissioner will not allow us to contact the subscribers again without two forms of consent?

* * *

---

* For instance: are security costs for candidates part of the campaign budget? At first, the answer was no. Candidates had to be protected. Later, it was found that security costs were only excluded if the funds paying for them came from public money. It could have led to a major breach of spending limits.

Data handling had changed a lot and suddenly. Very few of us were fully aware of the new data protection regulations. This document of ninety-nine articles and 50,000 words had arrived from Brussels and become compulsory the year before. It 'shall be binding in its entirety and directly applicable in all Member States', it said. The effects of the GDPR, like everything from Brussels, were tidal in their extent, flowing, as Lord Denning put it 'into the estuaries and up the rivers'. It certainly nearly swamped our early administration.

Considering the reputation of the Brexit Party among the Remaining classes, it was important our database of supporters was secure. I asked Phil whether people were actually trying to break into our system. He said, 'Andrew. All the time.'

We needed a hyper-professional set-up.

Consider the pitch we had from a data protection specialist. We had been quoted £20,000 for the building of a supporters database, two lots of hosting and back-up, weekly updates and 'refresh', 'data selection' and 'extraction'. Already, you feel, most people my age would be at sea with some of these terms.

Was the pitch company trading on our lack of knowledge? Maybe – but they would certainly be effective in striking fear into the heart of any political organisation. They said, 'Apart from any reputational damage, breaches of the Data Protection Act can entail a fine of 4 per cent of turnover for each breach.' *Each* breach? 'A determined hacker might cause 100,000 such breaches, resulting in accumulating penalties.'

The suggestion left in the prospective client's head was that unless we hired these people, we might be up for fines totalling 400,000 per cent of our turnover – a sum approaching the GDP of Norway. We had backers, but no one with the depth of pocket of an oil-rich nation with a sovereign wealth fund.

After the initial shock, we understood it was a compelling sales tactic. We used someone else, in the end. But his last point resonated with us: the Brexit Party was a 'high risk organisation for individuals wanting to use data protection as a malicious tool'.

Our opponents had adapted to and kept up with advances in technology far better than we had. They understood how to use it to their advantage in ways great and small. One individual, hoping to overload our system, sent as his email address the entire text of *The Hobbit*. Others joined up as supporters, then immediately resigned for some supposedly legitimate reason and demanded their money be refunded. We discovered we weren't able to make refunds with our initial-stage systems.

Early on, we received a subject access request. This part of the regulation gives anyone who appears in your database the right to interrogate your system for the information that is held on them. Fair enough, you think, and you're probably right. But in the hands of a hostile inquisitor it was a cunning way of gumming up our works. The individual asked forty-one questions that by law required an answer. The questions (downloaded from the internet) were arcane. 'What country are your servers located in?' was the least of it. 'What are your disaster recovery plans in the event of a crash, or a data breach?' We had to be able to report things like, 'Data relating to your visit(s) to our site will have been shared with the following cookie providers…' I had – and have – no idea what a 'cookie provider' is. And, even less intelligibly, we informed our anxious inquisitor that we had 'preserved user session state page requests with PHPSESSID'.

You have to take much on trust in the modern world. I don't think anyone I have ever had for dinner at my house knew whether 'user session state page requests' meant anything or not.

The tactic is clever. It demands at minimum that the target organisation employs a data specialist to handle that side of things. The costs are such that you'll need to raise over £100,000 a year to cover the expense of, among other things, a policy, a request form, a privacy notice and a request log. And, obviously, an incident management plan (£897). We needed a profanity check and something called ping testing. We had to have documented and mitigated any risks associated with processors – the data handlers beyond our control that we would have to identify and review. We had to ensure that processing of personal information only takes place in 'adequate' countries. The website should be assessed for vulnerability to cyber-attack. And of course, staff need to be trained in the intricacies of data obligations.

It was – is – a mass of unsuspected intricacies.

The subject access requests were a particular case in point. They came in at a trickle and we became accustomed to dealing with them, using a template. But then we sent out our 27 million election leaflets and we had 700 requests come in over a few days. Sackloads of them, five bulging mail bags demanding any amount of data protection information. It didn't matter that they weren't entitled to the information (the mailshot had been part of the normal political process and their addresses had been accessed via the electoral roll). We couldn't throw the sacks away; the hostile mail was mixed in with our regular post – applications, cheques, enquiries. Each sack had to be emptied, inspected, sorted.

And how do you manage that emptying and inspecting if you're running a lean organisation? Everyone is over-committed. The treasury staff are working until 9 p.m. every night. You have to call in temps to clear the load. But if you hire ten unscreened temps, you can bet that among them will be at least one undercover journalist or one agent for Remain or one anarchist or Marxist or general saboteur. And who's going to screen the applicants?

AN EVEN ROUGHER OLD GAME

* * *

There were other tactics that had come into being over the previous five years. They had gone beyond putting talcum powder into the envelope and hoping it would be mistaken for anthrax. Opponents had taken to making small but impermissible donations that would, if accepted and discovered, count against us with the Electoral Commission. It is, after all, a criminal offence to accept impermissible donations. All had to be checked carefully. Apart from anything else, there are fines of up to £20,000 or even jail at stake. The Electoral Commission showed itself to be assiduous in pursuing irregularities, as when it went after young Darren Grimes for ticking the wrong box of his registration form. They fined him the maximum £20,000 and, according to Darren, spent £500,000 fighting his appeal against the fine. It is an even rougher old game when the referee is not just hostile but armed, and not just armed but trigger-happy.

We made great efforts to keep within the rules and our opponents made even greater efforts to lure us into transgressions.

One fellow calling himself Nicholas Buchanan launched an eccentric but momentarily effective operation on the basis of denouncing himself for having made impermissible donations.

We received this email the day before the European elections:

From Nicholas Buchanan
To who [*sic*] it may concern
I have donated over three times through your website. All three times I have donated £500+ and have donated with international details and with an international bank account linked to an international PayPal account. Two of these are Russian/Ex-Soviet based. Can you explain how my donations were accepted and have been included with your funds? I eagerly await your reply. I have screenshots of the entire process, proof of international residence for the donation, proof of funds being transferred and acceptance of my donation. I would be keen to here [*sic*] how you will remedy this. Best, NDB.

Our first thought was that Mr Buchanan had entered into a conspiracy to break the law and that we should report him to the Electoral Commission. And only after an interval did we wonder how Mr Buchanan had made these donations, as PayPal could only receive sums under £500.

It was in this final check that we realised the whole thing was nonsense. Nicholas Buchanan didn't exist on our database and probably didn't exist at all. He had made no donations. His purpose was to soak up administrative time and distract us from our purposes. After we had reported it to the Electoral Commission, we were left with the distinct impression that somehow, even though we had ourselves reported it, we had been tarred with Buchanan's wrongdoing.

Phil wrote to the Commission's financial reporting manager laying out the circumstances. That the PayPal account could not accept payments over £500. That Nicholas Buchanan had never in his own name or from his email address made a payment to the party. That from his own statement he had committed an offence under the Political Parties, Elections and Referendums Act 2000 (PPERA) and the Commission should report him to the police.

The Commission replied by repeating much of what Phil had just reported to them, but in their best tutorial tone:

> As you are aware, a donation received by a registered party must not be accepted by the party if the donor is not a permissible donor, or the party is not able to ascertain the identity of that person. If you receive a donation which you are prohibited from accepting you must either return it or forfeit it within the relevant time limit.

There followed a full page of irrelevant and irritating advice – considering that no payments had been made – finishing with, 'You will need to decide whether to accept, return or forfeit the donations.' And the supremely useless, 'If you wish to refer this matter to the police that is of course action you may choose to do yourself.'

All these tricks and scams were played on us before and during the campaign proper. Here are a number of others that you generally learn by bitter experience:

- If you advertise a campaign rally with free but bookable seats, your opponents may book as many seats as they can and then not turn up. They are hoping that the media will be able to photograph swathes of empty seats and conclude you have no public appeal. As this tweet suggests, 'UCNUT (Warning – Fascism) Please don't book tickets for any of these events and then fail to turn up. It would be embarrassing if half the seats were empty.'
- If you book a venue for a rally or even a meeting, have a Plan B. The owners of the venue may be ardent Remainers and only accept your booking in order to cancel it the day before the event. Absurd? Impossible? It happened to us twice. The second time we had rung the week before to confirm the booking at a racecourse and all was well. Then the day before they emailed us to say they were withdrawing the booking. They relied, perfectly legally, on a clause in the fine print that allowed them to cancel 'if circumstances changed'. A rally costs a party between £30,000 and £50,000 but only around £4,000 for the venue. A last-minute cancellation causes the party much more pain than it causes the venue.

- If you mail out with paid-for return postage, a certain number of opponents will mail you back a brick (you pay the return postage according to the weight of the package).
- Among any 100,000 supporters, around 500 of them will be 'malicious actors'. That is, people who will do what they can to disrupt your systems, gum up your works, bring you into disrepute if they can. They might send you a cheque for 1p, in the hope that you will process it at the bank and take up administrative time and effort. Latterly, a more ingenious method of disruption has arisen. People can send a 1p donation via your payment platform and then demand a refund. That throws a spanner in the works because in the early days you may not be entirely sure how refunds work, or that you are required to refund. Soon, you will find that the refund costs you over a pound in platform fees to administer, and this will please your opponents very much. It is possible to set a minimum level of contribution, but you will need to be thoughtful about how to present that – some of your base will not be well off, and even a pound may be a budget item for them.
- Your opponents may create fake Twitter profiles purporting to support you and then issue a stream of material they hope to associate you with – in the manner of: 'We must achieve Brexit so that we can set up concentration camps for illegal immigrants.' Everyone gets these malicious attacks. If you are anywhere to the right of *The Guardian*, you

will be accused of being fascists and the left will ignore any boundary of taste or fellow feeling to make the point. For instance, a Conservative poster had the headline, 'Let's stay on the road to a stronger economy.' A Labour councillor retweeted an image with the words transposed onto a railway track headed to an austere brick building with a tower. The councillor said she had not realised the altered version of the poster had used an image of the Auschwitz-Birkenau concentration camp.

- Opponents, if enterprising, may buy billboard space purporting to advertise your views. Led By Donkeys – a group of current and former Greenpeace employees – used billboards to present manifesto commitments they thought we would make. To reduce maternity pay. To introduce an insurance-based health service. Things that showed we were essentially a malevolent, anti-humanity organisation. It's unlikely any votes were won or lost by this venture, but it caused celebration among our opponents.

Other tactics are interesting insofar as they show the lengths that opponents will go to in order to cause the most trivial inconvenience. A supporter wrote to us saying:

> Something rather odd and potentially rather insidious has started to happen to me within a week of making my application to be considered as a candidate for the Brexit

Party. As I cannot for the life of me think who might want to be creating problems for me, I am wondering if the two events are in some way linked.

It was the start of a Sherlock Holmes story!

About two weeks ago I started getting calls from Muslims asking about prayers at a mosque in Barking, East London. I live in Bristol, nor am I a Muslim and have no connection whatsoever to this mosque. Initially I thought it was a simple misdial but I received a number of such calls and apparently, they were getting my number from a Google search for 'barking mosque'. When I took a look at it, in the details of the mosque on the right-hand side of the page that returns after entering that search, under the official London phone number was an entry in orange that said, 'A user suggests this phone number' and my mobile number was entered. I contacted the mosque who were quite helpful and got my number removed but they sent me an email saying this had happened to them before and they thought it was deliberate.

Tactical action may also be deployed against you by the media. An email was forwarded to my inbox saying, 'We've had a gentleman called Mark H***** ringing to say he wants to make a significant donation to the Party over a number of years (the figure of £40 million was mentioned).'

We never heard from him again. Maybe he was genuine, maybe he wasn't. But as a rule of thumb, big donors don't mention sums like that at first contact, over the phone. And £40 million would have been the largest political donation ever heard of.

I received an email from someone calling himself Kevin Bilston. It read:

From Kevin Bilston:

Hi,

We are interested in making our first ever substantial donation to a political party. We will be in London for the next three weeks. Are there any fund raising events being held? Our planned donation would be above the disclosure limit but in five figures.

Anne Elizabeth Grsovenor-Jay, pp Kevin Bilston

A five-figure sum promised by the boss of Anne Elizabeth Grosvenor? In these circumstances, it is important to take heed of the lesson provided by middle-aged men travelling on business. If a glamorous woman with a surname allied to the richest royal duke in Britain approaches such a person in a hotel bar, she is almost certainly not a moth drawn to his aura of mysterious power. He should assume, hard as it may be, that in spite of her wide eyes and generous curves her interest in him is entirely malevolent.

In this case, the trick was poorly framed. A PA to a serious businessperson does not begin an email with 'Hi'. Serious businesspeople have websites with several layers of pages. They have company addresses and landlines. They have an internet presence. Nor does the PA misspell her own surname. This was a poor attempt at entrapment. We felt we deserved better.

Provocateurs may also set up lookalike websites and do business with the public in your name. That is annoying and can be surprisingly difficult to counter. We had an early experience with one such individual, a classic of his kind. He had registered a Brexit Party website and accused us of passing off, i.e. Nigel was pretending to be this person, for monetary gain.

We're not here to make fun of anyone – but identifying the prose style of vexatious complainants may help others who find themselves targets of their modus operandi.

First, such characters arrive with a flourish, speaking with authority and certainty and making use of legal phrases and concepts in a slightly off way:

> Your registration of 'The Brexit Party' is a clear breach of my intellectual property – the same name and entity and is a common law tort of 'passing off'. If you continue to infringe my copyright © to The Brexit Party by passing off, then remedial action will be taken. The European Union is currently introducing new legislation on copyright theft

and the Commission take a very dim view of your theft of my intellectual property.

The Commission, as we know, consists of remote and god-like entities in the European firmament and is very unlikely to notice anything this individual wants to say to them. The inverted commas around 'passing off' and the emphasis given by using the © after the word 'copyright' was another sign that he was acting outside his circumference.

You either come to terms or conflict will ensue. I do NOT allow anyone to steal my property and get away with it.
Thanking you in anticipation.

The heroic assertion is very much part of the psychology and the anti-climax of 'thanking you in anticipation' adds a comic dimension to his profile.

This person had registered his name The Brexit Party with an organisation called Copyright House, which offers a service to artists, writers and musicians. Register your work with them, their pitch goes, and you will be able to prove yourself to be the originator of the work in question. Unfortunately, it doesn't provide protection for trademarks, which is what our friend was after. That is granted by another body altogether. Nor is there copyright in a name, particularly not in one using such common words as Brexit and Party.

His next move carried a little more weight with me because I knew next to nothing about internet protocols. He sent us a letter saying: 'Please see attached DMCA Take Down Notice … reported directly to your domain host at Google Domains.' Was this possible? A takedown notice – was it credible? I had no feeling for it.

Taking down our website would cause a hiatus in our supporters' contributions, which were coming in at the rate of thousands of pounds an hour. It's the sort of claim that gives you a shock, when you realise it might constitute an existential threat. But even without knowing what a DMCA was, I felt his way of expressing himself suggested he was not to be taken seriously. This feeling was given substance when we found he had a presence elsewhere on the internet. He had been found guilty of criminal harassment through publishing 'grossly offensive' tweets and referring repeatedly to a young woman as a neo-Nazi. Part of his defence relied on this novel legal idea: it was inaccurate to state that he owned the offensive blogsite because it was owned by the online publishing platform WordPress. He was sentenced to six months in prison. His reaction was to complain to the press regulator. (The address given for him wasn't his but his mother's, where he was living at the time.)

Why didn't we ignore him? One's legal instincts kick in. They are deeply ingrained.

We sent him a letter saying that his use of the words 'Brexit

Party' was not subject to copyright. We also pointed out that the words had been in the public domain years before he had registered his name and that there was no general link between that and the Brexit Party because nobody had ever heard of him except those who had read of his court case in their local paper.

Perhaps it was a little heavy-handed, but it was very much enjoyed by this individual, who replied within the half-hour:

> I was expecting exactly that type of ridiculous and insulting response and it does not surprise me ... your evil former employee Sarah Grieves* knew all about the Brexit Party I had created ... hideously evil ... falsified allegations against me to the Dorset police ... all crooked and incurable liars like you ... parasite Tories on the make ... former UKIP whores still whores ... Jacob Rees Mogg ... As for your threats I laugh at them, you're a little boy in the scheme of things and I will ignore them ... Therefore, if you want a battle, good, you've come to the right man and I'll give you a battle like something you could never imagine.

He finished by informing us he would 'of course take out an interim injunction application to put your passing off

---

* Names have been changed to protect both the guilty and the innocent.

operation into protective withdrawal, followed by a delivering up application'.

We didn't manage to shut his website down until the elections were over.

The serious point was that this person really was passing himself off and taking donations from members of the public who thought they were donating to Nigel Farage. He was using our logo, our colour scheme and, as our supporters Facebook account manager told us, 'The message it gives is that the party is "anti-people", wants to privatise the NHS, is against increasing maternity pay, that people are generally wrong and stupid, that jihadi videos shouldn't be banned, etc. etc.'

We had many of our supporters writing to us about the fake site spreading misinformation. We contacted the site's hosting company to have it taken down.

This was two weeks before European election day. While the far-flung battle lines had been drawn up and Armageddon was about to be fought, we in head office were wrestling with a sad individual trying pass himself off as the Brexit Party. This is a whole level of politics that would-be politicians will have to transcend before they enter the Elysium of fighting for their great cause, whatever that might be.

On a scarcely more serious level, some months after the election we had a letter from a company called Trade Mark Direct who were acting for an entity called MKW and Sons whose registered office was in Twickenham. Google Street View can often cut grandiose threats down to size when the office is seen on screen, on a side street in a terrace of residential housing. MKW was said to own 'Brexit' and 'The Brexit Party' as trademarks for a variety of classes. They wanted to offer us a licensing agreement to use their trademarks and, to encourage us, threatened legal action for infringing their rights.

They had an actual point of leverage: we were applying for trademark registration ourselves. This action they were threatening, while without merit, could delay our application. It was not without a downside. How should such a problem be approached?

We researched them on the Companies House website and found that Trade Mark Direct and MKW had the same sole shareholder and director. They were inflating their presence to be more substantial, more threatening. The technique is well-known in the animal kingdom.

'It appears to us', our solicitors wrote in reply, 'that Mr K-W is personally procuring and directing the threat of infringement proceedings.' They went on into a four-page letter rebutting, refuting and making their own counter-threats. For any readers wishing to start their own political party, you will inevitably find yourselves faced with a similar action, so you may be able to construct your own legal letter by using these key points that Wedlake Bell made on our behalf:

- Under Section 21 of the Trade Marks Act 1994, unjustified threats are actionable at law.
- Your client has never used the trademark. How could he have signed the declaration that the company has a bona fide intention to use the trademark?
- The word Brexit has been described by the hearing officer as 'a very well-known term' with 'a very low degree of distinctiveness'. Registration has been declined and an appeal against that ruling has been dismissed. Your client's mark is likely to be declared invalid and therefore your case collapses. As you haven't used the mark there is no distinctiveness through use.
- We will seek indemnity costs.

We didn't take immediate action for an interesting reason. Had we done so, they could have objected to our application for the trademark (a process which was under way). Objection meant delay, and delay was not written into our schedule.

Such are the vicissitudes of a political campaign. You will notice that one important fact about them is the expense incurred by them all. All enemy action takes up management time and sometimes demands the attention of consultants.

Opponents will deliberately make life difficult, but friends can present problems of their own. Brexit supporters tend to be entrepreneurial of spirit and many of us run our own small businesses. The party regularly received propositions from other enterprises to give promotional items to supporters, or to sell Brexit-branded goods or give things away.

The key words to look out for are, 'I'm not interested in making a profit out of this (but obviously, I need to cover my costs).' This is always a sign that the project will be more trouble and probably more expensive than it is worth. A mail order fulfilment service carries with it all sorts of difficulties like storage, stocking, delivery, information processing, defaulting, angry customers and damage to the party.

It will save a world of pain if the party takes the attitude, 'We are not in the business of selling gin.' If the opportunities are genuinely there, the merchandising is better handled by a separate company.

* * *

One highly regrettable tactic has become more common these days. The threat of violence against politicians has increased and is increasing. Sometimes the results are tragic, as in Batley and Spen, where Labour's Jo Cox was brutally murdered in the street.

It's a sobering fact that the base car for Nigel, when he was doing his walkabouts, always had pints of saline solution and a supply of clinical gauze in case of acid attacks. There will be those reading these words and thinking, perhaps with a little shame, 'Nigel Farage would have to expect that.' But this new phenomenon affects politicians from across the political spectrum.

Nigel was getting all sorts of threatening emails. Some came from women convinced that Nigel was secretly in love with them. Others from men who were so convinced Nigel hated them that they wanted to kill him. Some of it was IRA-related, some of it from the extreme right, some of it from Islamists. 'I've never seen craziness like it,' George Cottrell says. Nigel's address had been published online by some administrative error of the council and it had been passed around activist groups. However, the postcode itself was a matter of dispute between local authorities as it lay on the border of two administrations, neither of which wanted the responsibility of protecting our man.

How serious were the threats? Only when UKIP emerged as an electoral force did the hurly-burly become something darker.

A woman at Lord's came up behind him after the match and poured a pint of lager over his head. Sounds comic? Sounds like something you'd shake off with a joke? You try it and see what it takes to keep that quizzical smile on your face.

When he went to his local pub with his children to meet his brother and his brother's children, he sent his security off for a couple of hours. The pub was targeted and demonstrators descended. The children ran out the back and hid in the cemetery behind the pub. When the adults got everyone into the car, the protesters were sitting on the bonnet to stop them driving off while others kicked in the side panels. 'They wrote the car off. They wrecked it. And you couldn't claim for it because you'd never get insured again.'

It wasn't long before he would not go into a building that didn't have a secondary way out. That's how things were developing. He would go into a pub and within ten minutes there'd be a flash mob outside, and very soon inside, shouting and jeering.

He'd been buffeted by hostile crowds in Scotland, hounded into the safety of a public building. He had things thrown at him – the eggs and the milkshakes you may have heard of. He was also hit hard on the back of the neck with a poster pole – a few centimetres lower might have paralysed him, such is the state of his vertebrae after the 2010 plane crash when he stood against Speaker Bercow. The security men at party conferences found and confiscated knives up to and including machetes. There's also a haul of paint pots, pepper sprays and one example of an anti-rape device that sprays a red dye into the face and can't be removed for two weeks.

How did he cope with these threats? 'It's like being around a big, dangerous dog. You mustn't show fear. But you mustn't display arrogance. What we most feared', he says, 'was acid attacks.'

There was a period when acid was a weapon of choice. It would be thrown in the faces of young women, mainly.

'Absolutely horrific thing to do to anyone. And then one of our security stopped and searched someone getting into our Glasgow conference. They found he was carrying a container of drain cleaner.'

We were lucky. But we were luckier because we were vigilant.

'We had a security number for the National Crime Agency and for the specialist unit that's responsible for Cabinet protection. We had a security detail drawn from the SAS and the SBS. They are very accomplished, very handy.'

Nigel says:

We never knew how much activity was going on. Nobody ever told us. We rang the Home Office frequently but never got anything useful from them, not ever. But then, six months after referendum night, I got a tap on my shoulder in Waitrose and a country-looking man said, 'You got me in trouble with the police a while back.'

He'd been out in the woods in front of our house culling deer at 4 a.m. with his rifle when six balaclava'd men with semi-automatic weapons held him up and questioned him. They were from one of the prevention agencies; they'd uncovered something of sufficient seriousness to get them to stake out the woods. We never heard of it at the time and never heard of it again.

George Cottrell says:

> Civil intelligence was something we lacked, but we knew there were active threats. Always. So yes, security has been of paramount concern. And 24-hour protection involves nine close protection officers and costs around £1 million a year. That's not something we wanted to apply for from the public purse. It was all paid out of donors' funds – and donors never had any problem coming up with the money.

And of course, there was always the tension between the press officers, who wanted uninterrupted views of Nigel coming down the central aisle of a conference – and the enormous security officers, who were hired to stand in the line of sight.

> And then with all the paraphernalia of a walkabout – you've got Nigel miked up for the social media clips and for contact with his private office. And when his phone went with an unfamiliar number from America, Nigel answered it and heard a voice saying, 'I am connecting you to the President of the United States.' There was an almighty scramble to get the various microphones off him – who knows how many people might have been listening in. And what they might have heard: Trump and Nigel Farage on the line in an unguarded conversation!

The serious point is that UKIP had been demonised. Thoroughly and comprehensively made out to be a repository of every backward attitude or dodgy political manoeuvre in the country.

'*The Times* was the worst,' Nigel says.

> Day after day, a constant stream of attacks on my life, my relationships, the party funding, the things UKIP councillors had said … You know, we had a lot of councillors who had said some pretty odd things in their careers. Many of them had been Tory councillors and had been saying the same odd things in complete obscurity. As soon as they joined the UKIP fold, the press put them into the national news. One particular individual joined UKIP and said – as he'd been saying for twenty years – that natural disasters were God's wrath delivered on us for gay marriage. No one paid any attention to him until he joined UKIP, and then he was two or three in the BBC news running order!

You can be forgiven for thinking that parts of the media really thought they could put us out of business. And there was evidence of their influence.

> There was a father in Southampton whose son's headmaster called him in. There was grave cause for concern. The

boy had been looking at things on the internet on a school computer. What was he looking at: porn? Bomb making? No, the boy had googled UKIP. And while you're laughing, take on board the fact that in the headmaster's study for this interview with the father the *police were in attendance*.

The media did a pretty good job on the whole Brexit tendency, but this was a new level.

'Norman Tebbit said to me in 2000,' Nigel says, '"CND was categorised as an organisation working against the national interest and the state mobilised against them. If you go on as you are – that's what will happen to you. You'll be classified as an enemy of the state."'

It's not to say that the media represented the state, but it came to be a distinction without much of a difference. 'They put a target on our backs, and we had to live with it. What else can you do?'

CHAPTER SIX

CHAOS IN THE COMMONS

I have neither eyes to see nor tongue to speak in this place but as this House is pleased to direct me whose servant I am here.
SPEAKER LENTHALL, 1642

I'm not in the business of invoking precedent.
SPEAKER BERCOW

Back at base, there we were, deep in the background, invisible, toiling in the darkness to work through these endless details that a new political party had to deal with.

And what was happening in the real world, as it's known – in the media, in Parliament, in the country? When Parliament came back from its Christmas recess at the start of 2019, never had there been such uncertainty in the Commons.

Brexit was rewriting the rules of party loyalty. A block of Tory Remainers had emerged – including Cabinet ministers – who would vote against the government. Many of us doubted the Prime Minister's commitment to delivering the UK from the Customs Union and the European Court of Justice – she was almost turning out to be a double agent. And finally, a new element had entered the game – that Lord of Misrule, Speaker Bercow.

Surveying the scene in Parliament, it was clear that all the normal rules of engagement had been abandoned.

That January, the sort of clean-break Brexit we wanted seemed to be more and more threatened. Brexit In Name Only was looking distinctly possible. The forces of Remain were gathering momentum. Their pressure groups were finding popular support and funding. The articulate middle class who had been humiliated by the rebuff to their authority were making ever-louder noises. They were high-profile, they were amplified by the media and they occupied positions of power and influence.

So, with the idea in mind that we had – just about – a functioning political party, let's see what was happening in the bear pit that Parliament had become.

In January and February, resolve on the right was softening. Theresa May's mini Project Fear was working wonders. The pressure point was this: 'If you don't vote for my Withdrawal Agreement, there will be no Brexit at all.' She argued that if her Bill was stymied, the demand for a second referendum would become irresistible. This had persuasive power in her party. Allowing a referendum that might overturn the previous vote was unthinkable to the Spartans, the group of Eurosceptic Tories who had vowed to fight to the death. By March, she was ready to throw in an added inducement. If the Agreement was passed, she'd resign. How sincere she was in that offer can never be tested.

Under the surface of all this, there was a huge opportunity for Labour. Some of the Spartans saw it and it was enough to shake them.

One of them put it like this:

If Corbyn had whipped Labour to vote for the Withdrawal Agreement, he could have destroyed the Conservative Party for a generation. Theresa May's Bill would have passed. The EU would have accepted it as the Exit, we would have been tied into their institutions, we would have had Brexit In Name Only. And then the anger of 17 million Leave voters would have destroyed the Conservative Party who had betrayed them.

It's a very good moment to realise how difficult politics is. The different possibilities politicians must evaluate, the options, the strategies, the consequences and unintended consequences. People who aren't involved – Man in Pub who wants to start the Enough Is Enough Party – have very little idea of the complexity of decisions and pressures on them.

For those who saw the opportunity for Labour it made us very nervous. If Corbyn saw the open goal in front of him and suddenly switched position and whipped his party into the Yes lobby...

But that didn't happen. On the day, Theresa May's Withdrawal Agreement suffered the largest government defeat in history.

But why were some of the Spartans voting *for* the Agreement? Brexit was never simple. Desmond Swayne was an ultra-Spartan and he voted for the Agreement.

On Swayne's account:

> We saw the whole thing going for a ball of chalk. It was the worst deal imaginable but we felt, maybe deluding ourselves, that we could sort it out down the track. If we didn't take what we were offered, we'd end up with the House taking control and passing a surrender Bill. There was no way of delivering Brexit with that parliament.

Did that mean Theresa May might get some form of her Agreement through, in the end? Was her threat of no Brexit genuinely powerful? It seemed to be so at the time, in all the smoke and fog of politics: yes, there was the possibility of Brexit never happening. We could still easily be sold out. If the Agreement was passed by Parliament, there would be no European elections. That would be the end of it.

An entirely new chaotic element was added to the mix. The Speaker's astonishing – brilliant – reinterpretation of the rulebook.

John Bercow (whom we all know) was the foremost procedural expert of his many parliaments. It was his technical supremacy that allowed him to create precedents over the Brexit period that shocked the small world of procedural experts.

He also understood the psychology of MPs, had a profound grasp of the power of the chair, and harboured a deep and abiding dislike of his former allies – Tories, Eurosceptics, Brexiteers, Nigel Farage.

He had delayed his exit from the Speakership in order to preside over Brexit. And here, from the vantage point of the Speaker's throne, all his knowledge, skill and passions were mobilised in the cause of Remain.

What he and his fellow Remainers must have seen was that the government could engineer a no-deal Brexit just by running down the clock. The PM could present her Withdrawal Bill and see it defeated once, twice, three times and the deadline would have passed. Their political enemies would have achieved the Holy Grail of Brexit – a departure on World Trade Organization terms.

Speaker Bercow had his own agenda as a result of his, no

doubt, honourably held beliefs. He sought to change the order of things so as to give himself a position not previously enjoyed by any Speaker. The government regularly puts up Business Motions in order to schedule debates and votes. The Speaker did this extraordinary, unprecedented thing. He allowed a Business Motion of the House to be amended.

Now, procedure in the House of Commons is as intricate and alien to me as the workings of the internet. In terms that are comprehensible by mortal mind, Speaker Bercow introduced this unusual procedure to allow Dominic Grieve to get his amendment voted on by the Commons. Grieve's amendment said that if Theresa May's Withdrawal Bill was voted down, she had to come back with a new agreement within three days instead of three weeks. The government wouldn't be able to run the clock down on Brexit, as Remainers feared was happening.

But what was controversial about this?

Amending a Business Motion was an interesting and unusual concept. The degree to which the Speaker appeared to be collaborating with MPs favourable to his political ideas – that was unprecedented. The idea that the House of Commons could intervene on government negotiations was so astonishing it took everyone by surprise.

Leave MP Peter Bone stood up and raised a point of order. He said had been to the Table Office in Parliament to ask if he could amend the Business Motion and been told that it was impossible. And yet here was Dominic Grieve's amendment on the Order Paper. It was unprecedented. This was backed up by Iain Duncan Smith:

> Over the past twenty-four or twenty-five years I have on a number of occasions, particularly during the Maastricht debates, asked the clerks whether we could amend a Business of the House Motion. I was always told categorically that precedent says it is not possible and, therefore, there was no point seeking to do so.

Speaker Bercow's defence consisted of three assertions:

1. That he was 'not in the business of invoking precedent';
2. That the Speaker's judgements are not questioned by Members;
3. That the order under discussion said the Motion would be put 'forthwith' – which means no debate but doesn't mean no amendments.

The argument went on for an hour on the floor of the House. Only procedural enthusiasts could follow it. Did a 'forthwith' Motion mean unamendable or undebatable? But an amendment could surely have no legislative effect? Only a minister could supplement the provisions of the order, couldn't they? Surely the Speaker was bound by a Motion of the House?

Ah but, the Speaker said, 'We are not treating here of a Motion but of an amendment to a Motion.'

'Further to that point of order, Mr Speaker!'

'No. There is no further.'

* * *

This was the first indication we had of the scale and depth of the Speaker's willingness to break from precedent. He was making it clear that he was more than an ordinary Speaker. Possibly he even came to see himself as the Prime Minister of the House of Commons (that really would have been a constitutional novelty). His supporters across the House, in many Brexit-related circumstances, formed a majority. John Bercow had personal power and he exercised it with ingenuity and force. After the European elections he would really get into his stride: the infamous Benn Act was still to come.

And all the time, outside Parliament, the possibility of a second referendum was still live. That was a project that caused us anxiety too. Every time a country had voted against the EU they had been invited to vote again. The second vote had almost always gone the EU's way. People's courage failed. That's what the organisers were counting on. They were encouraged by polling that said Britons were cooling on Brexit and that a massive majority of 2 million new voters, too young to have cast their vote in the referendum, would vote Remain.

Nigel was dubious about that. He operated on the understanding that only 4 per cent of that age group had contacted their MP about Brexit.

At any rate, we could see Parliament was locked and Brexit blocked. The second vote on Theresa May's Withdrawal Agreement suffered the fourth-largest defeat of any government Bill in the history of Parliament. Then the Speaker intervened with an even more impressive ruling. He invoked a centuries-old precedent that forbad her from presenting the same Bill, or substantially the same Bill, a second time. Some of us howled; others were left open-mouthed.

At least one thing was emerging in our favour: every setback for the government made an extension to the 29 March deadline more likely and increased the chances of holding the European elections.

As the weeks passed, Speaker Bercow's plan for the Commons to seize control of the negotiations went less well than his fellow Remainers might have hoped. The Commons isn't a negotiating body – it has many opinions and even among Remainers there were a skein of strategies all leading to slightly different versions of Remain. Bercow had given the House the power to vote for their preferred outcome, but there was no settled opinion as to what that preferred outcome might be.

The absolute state of the party of Remain was dramatised when the Speaker presided over eight indicative votes on eight different Brexit plans to find one they could all get behind.

Every plan was voted down. Even the idea of a second referendum failed.

The Speaker – as a great scholar of Parliament – might have understood the risk involved. When the government had put their various alternatives to the Commons regarding reform of the House of Lords a decade earlier, every one of them had been voted down.

One remarkable division did give some direction when the House voted to rule out no deal. The biggest card, the highest trump in the negotiators' hand, was the ability to walk away from the negotiating table. The Spelman Amendment, as it was known, was voted on (even though Caroline Spelman tried to withdraw it; the Speaker allowed it to proceed) and the Commons voted against invoking the only credible threat the British negotiators could make. It wasn't binding, but it gave aid and succour to the other side of the negotiation.

* * *

At the beginning of April Theresa May gave a press conference. We thought she was on her last legs because she hadn't anything to add to her position except to beg for unity. She wanted to pass her Bill 'so that the United Kingdom need not take part in the European parliamentary elections'.

We didn't like the sound of that. It would be a terrible anti-climax to our three months of round-the-clock work.

'Don't worry,' Nigel said. 'I think we're going to be all right.'

On 10 April there was planned an emergency summit in Brussels to consider a further extension – if Mrs May was going to ask for one. She wrote to the European Council. She asked President Donald Tusk to extend Brexit to the end of October, having pushed the deadline to 30 June only ten days earlier.

A day later, he agreed. 31 October it was. The European elections were in play. We were there.

CHAPTER SEVEN

THE SPIRIT OF IMPROVISATION

Your current media presence and increased fame is very exciting and we are all thrilled for you and many congratulations…! Sadly, however, politics (particularly at this turbulent time) cannot cross into the highly compliant world of education for healthcare professionals, organised and funded by pharmaceutical companies, and, hence, this decision taken by our client.
Dr David Bull forwards the notice of his sacking, after his employers found out he was standing as a candidate for the Brexit Party.

Truth be told, we weren't doing very well processing and selecting applications to be candidates.

The process of vetting potential candidates and selecting the right ones is of the highest importance. After the leader, the party's candidates are the next most important definition of what the party is.

Those of us from UKIP days knew very well how candidates could derail a campaign. In the world of political enthusiasts there are some very irregular opinions. David Cameron's characterisation of UKIP members as fruitcakes and loonies was unkind and in general wrong but, in fairness, not absolutely always misleading. All political parties have eccentric supporters. All parties harbour deplorables. It is nothing unique to parties like ours.

The danger is that certain eccentricities can become damaging if and when they are dragged into the spotlight. If someone with genuinely deplorable views is promoted into an official position by the party, there is a different level of exposure. A candidate has our endorsement. They represent us and our values. We are putting them into play with our brand on them. It is vital they truly represent us.

Background checks are essential but not always foolproof. In fact, the candidates' declarations weren't always proof either. In UKIP, a candidate read the pledge, 'I have never engaged in, advocated or condoned racist, violent, criminal or anti-democratic activity' and significantly altered the meaning of the sentence by crossing out the word 'criminal'. It wasn't picked up and he got through that vetting process.

To add to the complexity of the decision – what level of misdemeanour should disqualify a potential candidate?

If employment as a sex worker is not illegal, should that person be disqualified? Bankrupts are banned, but what about aged bankruptcies, where the individual has emerged back into the financial community? Having been convicted of a crime that attracted a criminal penalty? Surely, yes, that is going to exclude anyone. But should spent convictions count against a person? And how about someone who has a police caution – that new way innocent people have of escaping police custody but leaving a footprint behind? What about being on the police database logged as having been involved in a 'non-crime hate incident'? Should being associated with 'not a crime' be grounds for exclusion? Then there are adultery, stalking, eccentric sexual practices, family desertion, having been struck off a professional register – are these grounds for rejection?

There's a prior question that needs asking. How do you find out whether the applicants actually have any of these embarrassments attached to their name? One way – but it's not 100 per cent reliable – is to ask them.

I ramped up the questionnaire asking our thousands of applicants for details of their social media accounts, their letters to the editor, anything they published. We had to monitor their accounts on the basis that our opponents would certainly be doing so. But thousands of applicants had multiple ways of going wrong on their Twitter, Facebook and Instagram pages. Even in promising candidates you will find they have published ideas that sound viable only after twenty-five units of alcohol.

For instance, one of the UKIP candidates had posted an idea to solve the congestion problem in cities: benefit claimants shouldn't be allowed to drive. One of UKIP's senior elected members proposed that benefit claimants should be denied the vote. Another that everyone should only have one vote in their lives, at age fifty. It seemed to start a bidding war, as shown by this news article: "'Strip public of the vote,' says UKIP candidate ... "People who fought for the vote in 1832 and 1888 and so forth, trying to extend the franchise, were probably doing the wrong thing.'"

Compared with other opinions further down the scale, those were relatively respectable. I repeat, every party has these adherents – but it takes time to identify and discourage them.

One of our supporters and aspirant candidates felt she was born on Sirius, eight light years away. Another subscribed to the 'lizard people' theory about the royal family. Were we too sensitive when we found our Bournemouth office (in Pokesdown, it's worth saying) was the site of a former brothel and our regional organiser had been a popular dominatrix? True, she had narrowly saved us from adopting as a candidate a man convicted of starving 250 sheep to death, but was that enough of a character reference?

To use some examples from my UKIP days, one candidate looked perfectly sane and pleasant but was then reported for saying in some online forum, 'Only the Zionists could sacrifice their own in the gas chambers.' And, 'Have you noticed the stars on the $1 bill on the upper right corner, they make the shape of the Star of David.' That was a sign of the 'self-called prince of light, who in fact is the prince of darkness, or the "illuminated one"'.

These eccentrics may have been more of a presence in UKIP because the established parties had already expelled them.

My files boast an entry from the Midlands about 'a series of photographs that show [the candidate] naked, covered in vomit and excrement, clearly the result of being totally incapable following a drinking session'.

That certainly caught our attention. 'I have not seen these pictures', the local head of candidates went on, 'and despite requests have been told that the pictures have been destroyed as the taker of the pictures dropped his phone in the river…'

That candidate, incidentally, was outstanding and the slurs against him were dismissed. Office politics can be waged with a peculiar ferocity.

With all that experience behind us, we had developed a new automated system. It was computerised. It was, danger signal, a world-class new computer system.

What sort of advantage did that give us? We found out on the Friday before the deadline for filing candidates' nominations.

We had no candidates.

'What do you mean we've got no candidates?'

'We haven't processed any nomination papers.'

'*We haven't processed nomination papers?!*'

Without nomination papers submitted there was no Brexit Party presence on the ballot papers. These had to be submitted by noon the following Tuesday. Nor was it any Friday; it was Good Friday. And Monday was a bank holiday.

Parties select their candidates years before elections. We had ninety-six hours to process over a thousand applications.

The whole list of Brexit Party supporters had been emailed and each had been asked if they would consider standing as a candidate. We had decided to charge £100 per application. Despite that we had around 1,300 of them, all with extensive CVs filed in an online database with declarations that they hadn't got anything in their history that would embarrass the party or bring it into disrepute. No undischarged bankruptcies, no criminal record, no hate tweets, no membership of the BNP or the EDL. There wasn't a box saying, 'Do you believe floods are caused by gay marriage?' but we hoped we had already screened those opinion holders out. They had all to confirm the party's terms and conditions.

So far, so good.

It was calculated that if each CV was looked at by two people for five minutes each it would take a month to do the first sift. We could put a number of people onto it and get through the list in a week or so. It was in hand.

These calculations were now upset in time-honoured fashion. There was a row. Voices were raised. Regrettable things were said. The individual who had constructed the database left, closing the door behind him in such a way it was clear he wasn't coming back.

It was a while before it was discovered he had taken the key to the database with him. The new, world-class computerised system was rendered useless because it was locked. We couldn't get in. Nor could we get alternative experts to help – they wouldn't come. It was Good Friday and we were the Brexit Party and there was reputational damage in being associated with us.

It's a crucial rule for any organisation, but particularly in politics, where passions run high and regrettable opinions are forcefully expressed. When it comes to the computer system you must always be sure of a disaster recovery plan. Not just as a defence against a cyber-attack that eliminates your data – something much more basic. If your data team falls under a bus, you must have the entry requirements locked in a safe, preferably on an old-fashioned piece of paper.

So, there we were. Nomination closed in ninety-six hours. We had no candidates selected and no nomination papers completed.

It's the sort of situation that brings out the best in Nigel. After some brief but forceful expressions of disbelief, he gathered two or three of us into the office early on Easter

Saturday and we went through 1,300 applications by hand. They were printed out and processed manually, with the help of many pots of coffee and an undisclosed amount of alcohol. It was a victory of man over machine. I don't think I've ever seen Nigel quite so happy.

Realising the scale of the task was beyond us, we brought in a number of the regional teams from UKIP – about a dozen of them, all those we knew were of sound mind. Their knowledge and experience were invaluable. They knew the rogues. Without them we couldn't have done it. (The benefit of keeping on reasonable terms when you leave organisations.)

We ended up with an impressive slate of candidates. A decorated war hero, a retired rear-admiral, two ex-Revolutionary Communist Party members, the former editor of the original lad's mag *Loaded*, the former director general of the British Chambers of Commerce (forced out after he declared for Brexit), a high-up officer in the National Statistics hierarchy, Annunziata Rees-Mogg and, perhaps most impressive of all, a very late addition who called in over the weekend.

Nigel's phone went on the Sunday morning. 'Nigel?' the voice said with great clarity and conviction. 'This is Ann *Widdecombe.*'

Nigel didn't realise it at the time, but he had stood up, as if for royalty. She wanted to stand for the Brexit Party. Was she too late?

She was on a Saga-type cruise in the Norwegian fjords and

was due back on Tuesday morning, the very day nominations closed. Our head of candidates went down to Southampton to meet her boat at 6 a.m. on Tuesday and dashed the papers back to the Electoral Commission before the midday deadline.

We got them all in. All of them. Seventy-two candidates all signed, sealed, delivered before the bell tolled.

We were a month out from polling day.

The campaign opened the following week.

We were in hand. We were within the rules. We had our candidates.

* * *

The first thing to do was to prepare against success. Success can be more difficult to deal with than failure because the political psyche is a peculiar one. Topping a poll can unbalance the most grounded amateurs. And it is one of the most important qualities a would-be politician must have – the ability to keep their balance.

Imagine: you have been elected to public office. Your words take on added significance. Your views are sought by the media. You step onto a press conference podium and there is a crowd of upturned faces pointing at you. The spotlight is now shining on you and you are faced with the temptation to believe you have arrived at this political centre by your own efforts and under your own steam.

For these reasons, I developed a guidance agreement that each newly elected MEP would have to sign in order to prevent the most obvious disorders that might flourish in this new environment.

For instance, that the UK's exit from the EU was to be the focus for everyone elected under the Brexit Party banner. That was the foremost point. Also, that the MEPs elected were elected because of the Brexit Party – not because of their personal qualities. We felt it important to have them put their signatures to a document that stated in terms that they agreed their personal contribution was insignificant.

The head of delegation was to be in charge of any new ideas MEPs might come up with – and he or she was to clear them with the leader. It was emphasised that there was to be a Chief Whip and he or she was to be obeyed. Freelancing was forbidden. We also warned them about the dangers of journalists, of activists mounting sting operations, of the perils of attractive young women in bars expressing admiration for middle-aged men of substantial girth.

And finally, we wanted to alert them to the dangers of going native and submitting inflated expenses claims – as everyone else seemed to be doing it.

There was a campaign strategy, but speaking as a solicitor and far from a practising politician, such matters lie outside my circumference.

When one of our well-connected and highly experienced

recruits presented this as a campaign strategy, I didn't know what to make of it:

> What we want are seats where the Tory majority is bigger than the second-placed party, preferably Labour. Crudely, in these, if we can win more votes than half the 2017 majority, the seat should fall to us. The calculation we are looking for is where:
>
> Tory majority ÷ (Tory vote x the decimal of the Tory rump) = greater than 1.
>
> To flesh this out with an example, imagine a safe seat (where, for the sake of this illustration, the Labour vote stays the same) and we take 55 per cent of the Tory vote, leaving them a rump of 45 per cent, which is reflected as 0.45 below.
>
> Tory majority ÷ (Tory vote x (0.45) = ?
> = 15,000 ÷ (30,000 x 0.45)
> = 15,000 ÷ 13,500 = 1.11 = >1

It still makes me smile. The use of algebra must have a place somewhere in politics, but my guess is that it can be used to prove anything and the opposite of anything.

Ignoring the formal logic for the moment, the 2017 general election had Labour MPs in the Midlands saying they were finding a lot of Brexit support in their constituencies. Was that more important than the algebra? Was the UKIP vote going back to Labour or moving on to the Tories? Would the Lib Dems resurface in the south-east? Nigel had a nightmare vision (which may yet come to pass) of a Lib Dem resurgence that produces what he calls 'an orange wall from Uxbridge to Cornwall'. When the tectonic plates are shifting, algebra, or even logic, has its limitations. Experience creates instincts and long experience creates refined instincts. I left it to those who knew better.

* * *

One of the innovations Nigel had introduced derived from his contacts with the Five Star Movement in Italy. Modern parties had to look successful online. He didn't want us looking like amateur theatricals in the village hall. He realised we needed staging with slogans, boards, sound systems and camera techniques. Everything short of dry ice. The filming of an event projected the meeting far beyond the people in the hall – but only if the sound was good, the camerawork interesting and the editing good enough to create an effect of a pacy, exciting, modern event.

The events team had struck up a relationship with some young video talent who took their inspiration from filming raves – long, sweeping shots over the crowd. It created a completely different impression.

THE SPIRIT OF IMPROVISATION

The second rally we did as the Brexit Party was wilder than most because Bournemouth Council cancelled our venue the day before the rally. It's a trick our opponents used more than once. We had 1,000 people arrive in Bournemouth, all dressed up and nowhere to go. What could we do? Where could we go? A thousand people need facilities. There are regulations to abide by – fire exits, toilets, seating, a stage, lighting, power. A thousand people take a fair bit of accommodating.

Nigel knew someone who – amazingly – owned an airfield nearby, with a hangar. Within twenty-four hours, the team had got in raked seating and a makeshift stage, a sound system, signage, security – and far from collapsing in exhaustion, viewed it as a test run for the rest of the campaign.

Richard Tice remembers it for the first of the nasty protests. Racists! Fascists! *Nazi scum!* If you looked around, you'd think they must be talking about someone else. That really didn't match our voter profile at all.

It didn't help that the police were facilitating the protesters. That tends to be the case, we found out later, with protesters blocking traffic and stalling ambulances. But we all got in, the launch went ahead more successfully than it might otherwise have done and everything ran smoothly. 'Nigel's view was that the abuse was a sign the Brexit Party was being taken seriously,' Richard Tice says. It takes a solidity of character to find that silver lining.

Nigel's spirit of improvisation carried through into the events team working for him. In some ways, his modus operandi redefined politics as 'the art of the impossible'. One small example: Phil Basey remembers Nigel one mid-morning earlier in the year saying he was going to announce to a rally that they would be able to contribute to the cause via the website that was going up that afternoon. 'But there's still no donate button on the website, Nigel,' Phil reminded him.

'Well, there'd better be by five o'clock when I call for donations,' he said.

We had no website engineers lined up. The donate button had to be written into the code of the website and connected up to the receiving account in such a way that collected all the information that could be held to make us compliant with the Electoral Commission. You wouldn't believe it could be done in that time.

But there it was. By that evening, with two engineers paid treble time, the button was in place and connected to the financial processing back end.

As soon as Nigel announced it to the rally it started: *Ting! Ting! Ting-ting-ting!* Contributions came tumbling in. Was there enough bandwidth? Would the site collapse? There was, just. And it didn't, just.

In Norfolk, one of our meetings was massively oversubscribed. We found a second venue a mile away and directed the 150-person overflow from the village hall. Our two speakers took one hall each and at half-time they swapped ends. Nigel had a genius for improvising. He was unstoppable.

In the run-up to the elections we held rallies all over the country. Nigel said one Monday morning, 'We need a rally in Birmingham. A big one for 1,500 people.'

Right, it would be done, we had a team for it – there was a lot to do for a 1,500-seat rally. There was finding and booking the venue, there was marketing, advertising, banners, signage, insurance, security, stewards, fire marshals, hotel bookings, travel tickets, sign-up, and getting in 1,500 supporters.

And when did he want the rally to take place?

'Friday.'

'Which Friday? The first Friday next month?'

'Friday. Four days away. *Friday!*'

'It was bedlam,' Richard Tice says. 'Every day was a day of madness.'

* * *

Social media was said to have a great effect on the election. The people who say so are social media experts, so I take what they say with a pinch of salt. They say that Facebook and Twitter gain us converts – and it may be so. It's also true we may be preaching to the choir. Nobody can say for sure.

However, by any objective criteria, our social media campaign crushed the competition. The organisation 89up seem to be an authority on social media and have analysed the campaign.*

Here are some of their findings: the Brexit Party produced 13 per cent of all posts in the campaign but accounted for 51 per cent of all 'shares'. The Independent Group for Change spent £100,000 in a week on Facebook ads in the week before the vote and got the fewest shares of anyone.

Money is necessary but not sufficient. Remember, Michael Bloomberg spent $525 million on advertising in his failed campaign to become the Democratic presidential candidate. If no one's buying what you're selling, social media isn't enough to swing an election.

Leaving that aside, there are ways of getting your message out that don't depend on money. We generated forty-five times as many shares as The Independent Group for Change through shorter, simpler, stronger messaging and a deeper understanding of our audience.

89up also said that we at no point articulated our position on Brexit. That was a conscious decision. People wanted Brexit for many different reasons. We had communists and ex-communists, Labour voters, some Scottish nationalists and Tories voting for us as well as people as far to the right as the communists were to the left. If we went heavily on positions one, two or three, those who supported positions

---

* *The European Elections: How The Brexit Party won the online battle in the UK* by Ziad Ramley, Luke Rossiter and Mike Harris.

four, five and six would be alienated. The trick was to find the one rallying point and exclude everything else. In this case, it was simple. The cause was Brexit.

We gained more followers than every other party combined, attracted more comments than any other party and elicited more reactions than any other party. We posted half as many items as UKIP and gained 30,000 followers (while they lost 2,500).

We were, apparently, 'the undisputed winner on Facebook'. We got 324,000 Facebook shares, which was more than the shares of all other parties combined. We got almost the same number of Facebook video views as all the other parties put together.

On Twitter it was more of the same. We made up 9 per cent of the posts but generated 43 per cent of all retweets and 47 per cent of all likes. We gained 108,000 followers (again, more than every other party combined) and had an interaction rate an order of magnitude higher than any other party.

Let me ask a basic question. All that social media success – did it help? If so, in what way and how much did it help?

Social media proponents claim great things for their craft. They say they schedule their messages to go out at specific times – for right-wing voters, it is said that just before their dinner is the best time. They're low on blood sugar and susceptible to messages that will make them angry. Does that work?

Let's remember that the people who most loudly extol the merits of social media are very often social media executives whose promotion and pay depend on people believing their claims.

At any rate, by all measurable criteria, our campaign was a great success. Our messages were more heartfelt. They spoke directly to the emotions from which Leavers' opinions grew: the humiliation of the UK at the hands of the EU, the Tories and (crucially) Labour. It was a simple message we relied on: *your Labour MP wants a second referendum.*

The *Guardian* headline made sure to say that 'dozens of bots' were involved, as if that a) were true and b) could possibly have influenced things.

The question that new, insurgent parties will want to ask is: does the social media campaign convert voters — and if so, what do they convert them to? (Undecided to decided, decided to supporter, supporter to voter, for instance, are some of the divisions that will be of interest.)

For me, it's clearly true that social media can help to form a community of citizens who all believe similar things. And that by putting like-minded people in touch with each other, people can be shown that they aren't part of a weird, demonised minority but that many other sensible citizens believe as they do. It helps create a crowd — and as a crowd is the foundation of politics, social media must have a role. In a general election, however — where there are already deeply held loyalties and established cultural affinities – I have my doubts as to its importance.

There's nothing like campaigning on the ground – which is Nigel's natural environment. He turns up to a market town. He gives an interview to the local press first and then to any national papers that are there. He does a walkabout in the market, he visits the pubs. That's in the morning – in the afternoon he goes out of area to do the same again in a different media region. And then there's an event in the evening. He says, 'Nobody works the ground as hard as I do.' And that's true. His close staff who are at his side, his security, they keep up, but they're not broadcasting the gospel all day and half the night. That's the sort of performance over a month that puts lesser mortals in hospital with exhaustion.

On the last day of the campaign Nigel was whisked around the country and appeared in four of our target regions.

They were in Newcastle when a man in the crowd got close enough to throw a milkshake over him, spoiling his clothes.[*] They couldn't get to their chase car and jumped into the first taxi they found. George Cottrell, who comes from an elevated social background, said to the driver, 'Take us to the nearest clothes shop.' The driver suggested Primark. 'Primark! Is there a tailor around here?'

---

[*] The comedian Jo Brand said on a television programme, at a time when acid was being thrown: 'Why throw a milkshake when you could get some battery acid?'

'There's a gentlemen's outfitters,' the driver said, adding, 'but it's very expensive.'

They were able to meet the price for a new suit and shirt and were back in the front line before anyone had really noticed they were missing.

CHAPTER EIGHT

REMAINER DERANGEMENT SYNDROME

The party is at a high and ongoing risk of non-compliance with the Political Parties, Elections and Referendums Act (PPERA) with respect to its income.
ELECTORAL COMMISSION

There is little to assist me in the Commission's thought processes.
JUDGE DIGHT, IN THE DARREN GRIMES CASE

While Nigel was leading the party to a spectacular national victory through rallies, appearances and some soaring rhetoric, down in the engine room we were asking questions like, 'Has Form SR01 been sent to Companies House?' And, 'How do we demonstrate to the Electoral Commission what the law is on sub-£500 contributions?'

The Commission may have been observing the Farage effect out there in the country. They can't have been enjoying what they saw. A *Guardian* headline two weeks before polling day proclaimed, 'Poll surge for Brexit Party sparks panic among Tories and Labour.'

We were polling three times higher than the Conservatives. The paper stated that MPs feared Nigel would use the 'thumping victory' to back his argument that 'the UK must leave the EU immediately without a deal'.

There was a rearguard action.

On 20 May, three days before the polls opened, the Commission issued a masterpiece of innuendo. It might have been written for them by Remain's wiliest communications expert.

The press release began like this:

Commenting on reports about the Brexit Party's ability to ensure donations received via its website were from a permissible source, an Electoral Commission spokesperson said: 'The Brexit Party, like all registered political parties, has to comply with laws that require any donations it accepts of over £500 to be from a permissible source. It is also subject to rules for reporting donations, loans, campaign spending and end of year accounts. We have already been talking to the party about these issues.'

The implication was clear: the Brexit Party was suspected of

NOT complying with laws that require donations of over £500 to be from a permissible source. The fact that they had 'already been talking to the party about these issues' gave readers to understand that no satisfactory account had been rendered by us. We were under suspicion of crooked political financing – a criminal offence.

> As part of our active oversight and regulation of these rules, we are attending the Brexit Party's office tomorrow to conduct a review of the systems[*] it has in place to receive funds, including donations over £500 that have to be from the UK only.

Had a declaration like this ever been made before? Had the media ever been forewarned of a Commission visit to party offices, alerted so that they could send their cameras and reporters to fire questions at Commission officials as they left the building?

The innuendo was taken up readily by the BBC. Richard Tice went on the 7.10 slot of the *Today* programme to be asked in a characteristic way by Nick Robinson, 'Is it true you're taking money in all currencies including Russian?'

And note that other innuendo – 'donations over £500 that have to be from the UK only'. What was that but to suggest,

---

[*] A review, note, not an investigation. It is a distinction that has certain regulatory consequences. We never quite found out what they were. Someone's rear end had been covered.

slyly, that they suspected foreign money was being illegally accepted?

Bear in mind, they had no evidence that anything was amiss. They had been urged to do this by a letter from Gordon Brown (of which more to follow) and were acting on their unfounded conviction that there must be something fishy behind our success.

They finished with: 'If there's evidence that the law may have been broken, we will consider that in line with our Enforcement Policy.'

Just mentioning enforcement admits the possibility of enforcement – which inevitably blossoms in the media's hive mind to a probability, and among the ideologically driven to a certainty. 'The Brexit Party are being investigated for accepting illegal contributions to their campaign' is the takeaway message from that press release. Indeed, a Scottish MEP issued a slander (retracted under threat of legal action) saying, 'The Brexit Party is a shell company that's a money-laundering front.' In his apology he admitted there was no evidence for such a claim.

So, why was the Commission making this highly publicised visit to our offices right before the most important European elections the country had ever faced? Not but a week before they had told us they didn't have time to visit us before the elections. But suddenly, here they were, complete with media scrum boosting the party into the trawling tickers on 24-hour news channels.

How had that come about? There was one particular force at work. We didn't know at the time, but after a Freedom of Information request we found that Gordon Brown, the former Labour Prime Minister, had written to the Commission in his characteristic way:

Dear Mr Posner,

I am writing to the Electoral Commission and the authorities at the European Parliament to request that you investigate the sources of funding for the 'Brexit Party', and in particular whether any funding is coming from abroad and from whom – including whether any funding is coming from Russia – and whether proper and full declarations are being made in line with election rules.

There are immediate reasons why an investigation is now urgent and essential.

He went on to repeat a number of spent allegations against Nigel Farage and Arron Banks before returning to his meat:

Now Mr Farage heads the new 'Brexit Party', which is making questionable claims about the true source of its funding, especially claims about multiple, small, anonymous donations at a time when the Electoral Commission has warned of the dangers of such donations being a cover for dirty money. I understand that on their website the 'Brexit Party' are able to receive donations from foreign sources – even in foreign currency.

Given the Electoral Commission's duty to monitor every UK party's election finance and spending, it is important that we do not wait for months after the event to investigate dubious claims by a party with links to people who have been under investigation by you in the past.

The Commission had received this letter on the morning of 20 May. At 4 p.m. the same day they wrote to us requiring a meeting the following day at 9 a.m. This was giddyingly quick action from an organisation that required forty working days to consider a party's name change.

Nigel was flying off in a private jet with his staff for the start of his 24-hour, five-stop tour of the UK. They landed at Exeter Airport and as soon as the wheels touched down their phones started ringing. The news astonished them. Astounded them. It was far more serious than anyone on the outside had thought. The reputational damage was potentially ruinous.

How? We've seen how banks evaluate risks to their own reputation. If it became part of the accepted wisdom that we had been taking donations illegally from Russia then it was possible, or even probable, that banking institutions would suspend their services to us. Their risk managers would point out that they could be dragged into a regulatory investigation. They could be prosecuted for money laundering and be liable for enormous fines. It was a very severe case of defamation. Both Nigel and George Cottrell spent the drive from the airport on the phone to the three legal firms they had a relationship with – three of the top legal firms in London. All the senior partners they talked to refused to take the case on – in every case there was a conflict of interest.

If service was suspended, the party would have no ability to receive funds, to pay creditors; our cash would be frozen.

Isabel Oakeshott wrote a lively press release including the sentence: 'We are dismayed but not surprised by the Electoral Commission's willingness to dance to the tune of a handful of notorious left-wing agitators and a frustrated former premier.'

We felt it a little too strong to publish at the time and put this out instead: 'Our treasury is staffed with highly experienced, qualified, accredited personnel and we have a comprehensive set of internal procedures to guarantee full compliance with our regulator the Electoral Commission.'

To summarise: a political opponent had written an attack letter demanding action to a state body. As a result, the state body took the unprecedented action of releasing a media statement that they were investigating a political party and brought unspoken pressure on our bankers to suspend service.

Gordon Brown's letter was a masterful blend of smear and innuendo. 'Questionable claims about the true source of its funding', 'small, anonymous donations', 'dirty money' and 'even in foreign currency'.

I wasn't present at the meeting itself but was in constant phone contact with one of our officers. There had been a ruckus at the start of it. Feeling that the Commission was acting out of political pressure, that this was a stunt for the media, that we were being set up, that it was two days before the most vital elections, that we couldn't rely on what the Commission was going to say – for all these reasons, I suggested Gawain Towler bring his cameras in to record the meeting. Their reaction was volcanic. No one has ever seen studied, steady bureaucrats so out of sorts. That their 'here today, gone tomorrow' words might be permanently on the record flustered them out of their mandarin serenity – so much so that they began making threats of legal action via the Information Commissioner's Office. Were they aware that they had no basis for such a threat? To record any meeting is entirely legal as long as the visiting party is aware the recording is taking place. That is the legal position and these Commission officials are students of the law – that fact was surely known to them. It was an example of their making up rules and of issuing threats on the basis of their imaginary powers.

However agreeable it was to have the Commission on the back foot, they could do us great harm if they were provoked enough. They were a drowsy bear. 'Stop poking the bear!' was the advice that eventually prevailed. We even deleted what footage we had and deleted any transcripts that had been made. They didn't express any gratitude.

But to return to the meeting. When it finally started, we showed them the system we had of taking donations. We opened up our computers to them. They saw the money still coming in and the rate at which it was coming in.

Then we showed them the spreadsheet that recorded all payments received with a value of £500 or less. The spreadsheet contained 118,553 payments with a total value of £3,437,225 – all of which had been made by PayPal.

We also pointed out the number of multiple payers: there were sixty-seven out of nearly 120,000, an insignificant proportion.

The average payment was £29. On the face of it, there is no cause for concern in those figures. They don't flag up suspicious activity. No accountant would look at the data and demand a deeper interrogation of them. The Commission had already seen our system for flagging up multiple payments from the same email address.

The Commission treated it all, in George Brown's famous phrase, with a 'complete ignoral'.

There is nothing in the Commission's records to give an insight into their thinking. And it is impossible to look into their soul to pick out strands of motivation. But if you wanted to taint the victory of the Brexit Party – if you wanted to create a lingering impression that the vote was somehow illegitimate, the result of Russian 'bots' or of 'dirty', 'foreign' money – then this would be one way of trying to do so. Where the argument was raised that this remarkable vote by the British public was an endorsement of the referendum and could be taken as a proxy for a second referendum – opponents could say, 'Ah, but it was the Russians that made it possible.'

* * *

This was hardly the first battle we'd had with the Commission. For a quango staffed largely by Remainers, the Brexit movement was among their least favourite entities.

A decade before, UKIP's largest donor had let himself drop off the electoral register in England. He was resident offshore and was thus caught by regulations designed to exclude foreign influence on British elections. He was no foreigner, but the Commission took the strictest view and demanded the seizure of the donations he had made while he was off the register. The order would have bankrupted the party, destroyed it. A lower court agreed with the Commission and issued the order for seizure. We appealed and it went to the Supreme Court, where we succeeded by the narrowest majority of the seven judges.

In his common-sense reading of the law, Lord Phillips

noted that there was a distinction between 'inadvertent and deliberate failure to report a disclosable donation'. And Lord Kerr concluded the written judgment with the words: 'It was never intended that there be forfeiture in the true sense of that term where the donor was someone who was entitled to be on the electoral register but who was not registered because of an administrative error.'

It isn't paranoia to think we had been in their sights ever since. Other, culturally Remain, parties had always got an easier ride. The Liberal Democrats enjoyed exemption in this regard – when they were found to have illegally accepted a £2.4 million donation, they didn't even have to pay it back ('we've spent the money' was their successful plea).

More recently, we were all amazed when the new party created by Anna Soubry and Chuka Umunna, The Independent Group for Change (previously known as Change UK), had their party registration accepted by the Commission within twelve working days rather than the forty days on the Commission's website.

Mick McGough made a Freedom of Information request asking when they applied for registration and why the application had been accelerated. He gave the Commission the link to the page on their website advising party registrants to apply by early February to be in time for the European elections – the Remain-supporting party applied in April and had their registration fast-tracked.

The Commission replied that such a request was not considered a request for information under the Freedom of Information Act 2000 because 'a public authority is not required to respond to requests for an opinion, research, or to create information'. What a masterful bureaucratic phrase – they weren't obliged 'to create information'.

Mick pursued his point with the Commission, and many points thereafter. How could they call themselves Change UK when there had been a political campaigning group in existence for some years called Change? None of it gave them pause. He also told the Commission that the name was inappropriate as they were seeking, by their efforts, actively to resist change by staying in the EU. Status Quo UK would have been a more accurate name – although, granted, that might have created confusion of a different sort.

All these enquiries and objections were brushed aside, despite the obvious conflicts.

It's not as if the Commission lacks the power to rule out names on these grounds. Mick had been treasurer of the Tea Party for some years before the Commission deregistered it on the grounds that people might think the party was about tea.

As Mick pointed out, had we known this 'gold service' was available we would have dropped the 'The' from our name and risen to the top of the ballot paper, displacing Change UK. We might have gained an electoral advantage. On the other hand, it was also true that topping the ballot paper didn't help Change UK. Despite the presence of Rachel Johnson, Boris Johnson's sister, and Gavin Esler, the Man on the Telly, along with many other luminaries, Change UK beat UKIP by only 0.1 per cent and achieved 3.4 per cent of the vote. They won no seats and disbanded seven months later. A demonstration of the fact that it's the party that gets the vote, not the individual (except, of course, in the case of Nigel Farage).

That is an aside. More important to this story is the working relationship that had been established between the Brexit Party and the Commission. It was generally hostile in ways great and small.

Mick delivered some urgent papers by hand to the Commission's offices. The front desk refused to let him up to their floor. They refused to come down. The desk wouldn't give him a receipt. The documents were a change of officer form (which had a deadline on it) and the new constitution (also important). He was told to go around the back to the loading bay and the post room where he would be given a receipt. No receipt was issued by them nor sent in an email later, as promised. It is only a small example of the 'insolence of office' but characteristic of their corporate style. It is almost calculated to annoy. When we consulted a QC on the subject of the sub-£500 donations, the Commission wrote to us saying: 'We understand that your position stems from a misunderstanding of the law. We therefore invite you to share the advice from your Counsel in order that we might correct such misunderstanding.'

Our relations were established as master to the lowest servant from the start.

The bee in the Commission's bonnet really started buzzing when the news broke of the 100,000 supporters who had subscribed through our website in its first week. This started a legal and administrative argument which went on as long as the Brexit Party was in business.

An avalanche of money had flowed into the party's war chest. Almost all of it was in small amounts. Because the sums were under £500, they didn't have to be recorded, let alone reported. The law is clear on that. But the Commission blew an institutional fuse and felt they were being played. That we couldn't have got this money legitimately. That we needed multiple measures to satisfy them.

Why? On what basis? They wouldn't say.

For an organisation committed to transparency and impartiality, they are reticent, even paranoid, about how they come to decisions. As Judge Dight phrased it, upholding Darren Grimes's appeal against the Commission's £20,000 fine: 'There is little to assist me in the Commission's thought processes.'

What was motivating them? Was it a fierce regard for democratic values?

No other party had attracted this sort of attention. Was it a suspicion based on evidence of wrongdoing? They never produced any evidence. Was it a precautionary exercise to protect us from these all-powerful 'bots' that they claimed could be the basis of our support? They never produced any evidence that such bots existed or were able to use PayPal in this way.

So, what was in their minds? One of my colleagues attributed their behaviour to what is now the widely recognised 'Remainer Derangement Syndrome'.

They had received a terrible shock to their worldview from the referendum result. It was an additional shock when the Brexit Party attracted instant, enormous, unprecedented support from the public. From a standing start to 100,000 supporters in a week. No party had ever launched with such a result. For many Remainers it was literally unbelievable. They couldn't accept that ordinary, £25-a-time citizens were behind the surge. They were convinced the Russians must be funding us. That foreign nationals, impermissible donors, lawless oligarchs, gangsters and cartels were funding us with donation bots. The last people they thought could be funding us were the 17 million citizens who had voted for Brexit and who now felt that the Establishment was trying to foil it by process and procedure. The Brexit-supporting public understood the need to get a Brexit-oriented party into the European Parliament. With every important organ of the state against the project, the only way the public could participate was by voting. By supporting the Brexit Party with their £25 and by voting for it.

For those suffering from Remainer Derangement Syndrome, though, this was incomprehensible. The only explanation for our support was malign foreign influence. It couldn't possibly be ordinary citizens; it had to be big backers concealing their contributions by making multiple payments of £499.

There is one point we didn't like to make. It rendered fatuous the idea that we had big backers concealing their donations. The fact was (and I know that this sounds vainglorious) we were to have almost unlimited funds in the bank – declared, permissible, above board. Our major backer, a British businessman few had heard of, was to make us the largest donation in UK political history.

Did we need the smaller donations? We certainly did – we made good use of the money. But the money wasn't the point in itself. When citizens give, it strengthens their commitment to the cause. It makes them more likely to vote and more likely to become active on behalf of the cause.

But we always knew we had to stay scrupulously within the regulations. We knew we would get no mercy from the Commission or the media. We made every effort to persuade them we were taking all reasonable action and as a result we commissioned a QC to give us an opinion (such advice comes at the rate of £5,000, for those interested in such matters). He confirmed our legal reading of the Act.

Our understanding of the regulations was this:

1. Donations have to come from permissible donors. Usually, that meant the donor had to be on the electoral roll in the UK, whether or not they were resident in this country (there are a lot of expatriates living around the world).
2. Any donation over £7,500 has to be reported. Multiple donations that accumulate to more than £7,500 also have to be reported.
3. However – the big however – donations under £500 were not considered donations and could be disregarded. It says that in black letter law. 'Any donation whose value is not more than £500 *is to be disregarded*,' our QC quoted from the statute. He went on to say that the draftsman knew very well what he was doing because he spelt out a way in which people might try to get around his regulations by finagling trust donations. The QC wrote: 'There is nothing in the provisions surveyed to suggest that donations whose value is not more than £500 ... are to be aggregated where the donation comes from the same source. To read in such a requirement in circumstances where the draftsman has been meticulous in setting out provisions to prevent circumvention defies basic principles of statutory interpretation.'

There are many qualifications and elaborations in the 'permissible' section of the Act. For instance, if the donation is more than £7,500, the person donating it must give their full name and address.

Nowhere does it say people making smaller donations should give their name and address. If circumstances were being considered at this level of detail, it is inconceivable that the drafters would not have made explicit that donations aggregating to more than £500 should be considered as one donation.

In summary, we said, 'Donations to political parties and non-party campaigners of £500 or less are outside the legal donation framework of the Political Parties, Elections and Referendums Act 2000. And that means that there is no legal requirement for these donations to be reported to the Electoral Commission.'

The Commission's position was way wide of this. They said and kept saying, 'The party is at a high and ongoing risk of non-compliance with PPERA with respect to its income.'

And they would add more powder to the charge by saying, 'It is an offence to attempt to evade the controls on donations. This includes where it appears that a donor is attempting to evade the rules set out in PPERA by making a series of small donations.'

Nowhere in the Act do these words appear – 'a series of small donations'.

Mick McGough, in fact, had a system of checking whether multiple donations had been made. There had been two or three but nothing significant. Phil Basey, the next treasurer, had his own system, which he exposed in full to the Commission. Here is his account of it:

1. Our PayPal account cannot accept payments over £500.
2. The party has only ever accepted two payments over £500 before the limit was imposed. They were received on 8 and 9 February and both were for £1,000. One payment was from a UK company which was checked out and accepted; the other, from an individual, could not be confirmed so was returned.
3. The return was entered on the party's first quarter return to the Commission.
4. The Commission were shown proof of the return within thirty days.
5. I built an analytical model of the PayPal data that aggregates multiple payments from the same person (via an email address).
6. This model isolates collective payments over £500 and shows any pattern of payments that may be an attempt to evade PPERA.
7. The model was demonstrated to the Commission and their advice sought as per their guidelines.

We have no record of the Electoral Commission offering us their evaluation of this system. They ignored it. They merely said that we had no system.

We had opened up the banking screen and let them play with the system as much as they wanted to. Thousands of pounds a day were still pouring in from our supporters. We told the Commission how we had brought journalist Dave Wooding in to interrogate the system. He took a more active interest in the system than the Electoral Commission and found nothing to scandalise about.

Our third treasurer, Mehrtash A'zami, who took over when Phil's blood pressure crested 220, evolved an even more elaborate system.

In the first place we had the donor's email as the unique identifier of an individual's donation. Mehrtash used a 'pivot table' to repurpose our spreadsheet of donors into a database we could interrogate for multiple donations.

But nothing pleased the Commission. Even though Mehrtash had us audited by Wilkins Kennedy, one of the top ten accountancy firms, they continued their investigations into us for two full years after this point. Eventually they found that four or five invoices – all for small amounts – hadn't been paid within the sixty-day post-election limit and they fined us £200. That was a very poor return on two years of investigation into £7 million of donations. But it may have had a desired result for Remainers in that it gummed up our works by adding cost and diverting resources from our goal. Mehrtash says:

We had been cleared by an audit of our accounts, but then, right in the middle of a general election, the Electoral Commission were asking for copies of this and documents about that for days and days. And all around everything was moving at three times the speed you are used to in normal life.

Mehrtash had an admirable instinct to adopt a conciliatory attitude to the Commission. His rationale was that these officials were permanent features of the landscape and their hostility would endure beyond any local or temporary confrontation. I had my doubts whether conciliation would produce any better results than our energetic skirmishing. I advised him, 'They will never be your friends.' And indeed, they never were.

* * *

One skirmish in our thirty-month bureaucratic battle came directly after the European elections.

In an email sent after the meeting, the Commission's head of registration set out their definitive corporate view on the £500 limit and the possibility of multiple donations. This was the only time they went into detail, and from the prose we may be able to see why they hadn't done so before.

The argument doesn't bear scrutiny.

The head of registration began with this affirmative statement: 'The recommendations we made that relate to payments of £500 or under are appropriate on the following basis.'

Good, let's hear it. The Electoral Commission's official position. She said: 'Whether something is a donation as defined by PPERA is a matter of fact. For example, if an individual gives £200 a day for a week, whether it is seven separate payments or one donation of £1,400 will depend on the facts.'

This is not a legal reading; it is free association. 'The party should be reviewing circumstances where one payer has made multiple payments of £500 or under that add up to over £500 to determine whether it is in fact one donation under PPERA that has been broken down into multiple payments.'

She tells us that seven separate payments could be considered one payment depending on 'the facts'. But what these facts might be she did not say – and would not say for another six months.

She laid on us the duty to 'review the circumstances' but gave no indication of what 'the circumstances' might be or how they should be assessed. Is a monthly subscription of £50 one donation or twelve over the year? Would a pensioner's multiple contributions be assessed differently from a corporation's? Over what period are the amounts to be aggregated? What happens when the donor has moved address between donations – what steps must the party take to identify the donor as being the same? What circumstances are relevant? What are these 'facts' that should be reviewed? No one would be any the wiser from this statement of the Commission's position.

Her second argument was not just insubstantial; it was irrelevant. She said:

> Section 61 of PPERA sets out offences concerned with the evasion of restrictions on donations. It is important that the party has systems in place to manage the risk of them being used as a vehicle for such evasion and to be able to identify if this has happened and take appropriate steps.

She does not quote the words of Section 61, perhaps because they did not help her case.

There are two parts to Section 61:

1. The first makes it a criminal act to knowingly facilitate a donation from a donor who is not permissible. (Essentially, the permissibility of the donor has nothing to do with the question of a £500 limit. Also, the word 'knowingly' carries a lot of weight in that sentence.)
2. And the second is aimed at the person making the donation, not the party. The donor is liable for the offence.

That, in a nutshell, is why Section 61 has no bearing on the argument she is attempting to make. She tries to make it stick by inventing a new duty for the party – transferring responsibility for the donation from the individual to the party. That responsibility is not in the wording of the Act. It is another example of the Commission extending its powers. Their wings would be clipped the following year, but they were at this time still flexing their administrative muscles.

They made no attempt to engage with our arguments or with the wording of the Act – they simply reiterated their position, which, in our view, had no substance.

This running battle was very serious from a party point of view. If the Commission had a strategy to disallow our supporters' contributions by some administrative trick, it would have been a huge threat to us. Over the year their demands escalated. They wanted us to put a CAPTCHA device into the donations process to eliminate the possibility of donations from these phantom financial bots that were apparently capable of making multiple payments from the same PayPal account.

If the Russians wanted to funnel money into a favoured operation, there are infinitely easier ways to do it – especially if there are direct economic benefits in so doing. For example, various environmental groups in this country agitate against the UK developing its own gas resources. This limits our potential for energy independence. It makes us more dependent on gas imports – most of which originate in Russia. If there isn't Russian money in our environmental organisations, I would be very surprised, given the immediate economic incentive. But this is by the way.

Two years after this accusation of Russian bots funding the Brexit Party, Mick sent the Commission a Freedom of Information request. He asked: 'What evidence does the Commission have of any political party being in part funded by bots making multiple payments, in order to circumvent disclosure requirements for donations over £500?'

They replied: 'We hold no evidence that any political party is being financed, in whole or part, by bots making multiple donations, or any donations at all.'

No evidence? The Electoral Commission admits having no evidence at all that bots were involved? But bots had been a key plank in their case against us. We were pilloried for having had no system in place to detect bot activity.

And now it is clear that the Commission had no idea of how bots worked, no real idea of what they were and no evidence that they existed.

In addition to this, PayPal has sophisticated fraud detection procedures in place, in order to protect their business model. The risks posed to a payment processor are from fraudulent payments (which in some cases take up to 180 days to be known) where they, the processors themselves, become responsible for issuing the refunds. It is obviously in PayPal's interests to have the best possible fraud detection technologies.

These include scoring the behaviour of the customer via IP

address and location, device, time zone, keyboard language, name, address, card issuer country, transaction currency and email address. (Possibly also collecting telephone number, proof of address and government-issued photo ID when creating a PayPal account, where details haven't been automatically confirmed against data sources such as the electoral roll, credit reference agencies etc.)

The degree of sophistication to spoof all of this information – plus much more which isn't public knowledge – would be hugely expensive and uneconomical given the average transaction value of £25.

Yes, on occasion a bad actor, prankster, political activist or journalist may be able to circumvent these procedures by creating two, possibly three or four PayPal accounts, but they would be in breach of the terms and conditions of PayPal and the Brexit Party by knowingly giving false information, which would also constitute an act of fraud.

At the time of the election, we were lucky to have George Cottrell on board, who knew more about these matters than most. He was able to penetrate the financial systems to ensure there were no irregularities.

George says:

Every incentive we had was to comply with the regulations: accepting impermissible donations would have been a disaster. And coming from the other side, there was never a shortage of money. We didn't need to bend any rules.

The whole over-zealous strategy of the Electoral Commission was based on a stupid misconception – that we would connive in breaking the law and risk existential damage to our cause for the sake of a few thousand pounds.

We felt that the Commission's board consisted of Remainers and hence the institution was infused with the spirit of Remain; that they would prefer to help Remain-oriented parties; that they would strictly regulate parties working for Brexit; that they reacted to gossip and slurs promulgated by senior politicians; and that they lacked the impartiality of a state body created by statute to supervise democratic functions.

These things may not have been obvious to anyone away from the line of fire. To us, on whom their guns were trained – there was no doubt about it.

To have a media scrum outside our offices two days before crucial elections, speculating about political gossip that we were receiving illegal donations from Russia, and all on the instigation of a former Labour Prime Minister – this was how much a state body had become politicised on one of the greatest issues of the day.

But it didn't affect the result. Despite the Commission's

involvement, Act One of the Brexit Party was to end on a great climax.

CHAPTER NINE

A DIFFICULT DECISION

Like all victories, it comes with regrets.
NIGEL FARAGE

The European elections were the Brexit Party's high point – a success that was only possible under a system of proportional representation. And what a high it was. The British public had reaffirmed their commitment to Brexit. In the absence of a second referendum, we felt this was as close as anyone could get to an affirmation that the will to leave the European Union was still there, unabated.

Voting support from the public, when it happens, is unlike anything else in political life. The rush as the results came through – if you've ever felt the wind beneath your wings, you'll have an idea of the feelings we had. The party's supporters feel it as a vindication of everything they believe. It's a huge 'hear, hear' from the country. The political heart soars.

Add to that, the polls were making astonishing projections for our new party. First, that the Brexit Party would be the next government and second, that the Conservative Party would be reduced to twenty-six seats.

It's important in these exhilarating occasions to keep your balance because these predictions were obviously worthless.

Nigel was the first to warn against hubris. He said, laughing, 'The Conservative Party hasn't been the dominant party in Britain for 200 years for nothing.'

We did think, though – we did dream a little – that the Brexit Party might evolve into a full-spectrum party representing the common-sense middle ground.

Something of the Tories' operational ruthlessness was recovered by the party in the week of the European elections, as was seen in the fate of Prime Minister May. The Tories had been absolutely crushed in the result. They had won a mere four seats across the UK – four out of seventy-three. The week of the election, Theresa May had announced an initiative to get her agreement through Parliament. It had been worse than anything we'd seen before. Her new Brexit deal promised, among other things, a vote on whether to adopt a temporary customs union and a vote on a second referendum.

Her Cabinet denounced it, and by her account, she didn't

even believe in it herself: 'I think we should be implementing the result of the first referendum, not asking the British people to vote in a second one.'

Such were the words of a Prime Minister who had completely lost her way. The Leader of the Commons resigned rather than present the Bill, but still the PM clung to her position.

Both wings of her party were scathing.

'This is a betrayal of the 2016 referendum and a betrayal of everything she has been saying since she became Prime Minister,' Tory MP Robert Halfon said.

Still she clung on, through Wednesday and Thursday of election week, her authority collapsing around her. She met with the chair of the 1922 Committee of backbench Conservative MPs and was told that she would be ousted immediately if she didn't go of her own accord. And the reason was an interesting one, as we'll see in the conclusion of this book. The particular impetus behind her fall was that sitting Tory MPs were spooked. They saw clearly that they would lose their seats if this went on. Their only route to survival was conditional on the demise of their leader.

The Brexit Party had done what it had been set up to do. We had shown the negotiators that the country's appetite for Brexit was undimmed. Or, indeed, intensified. Our polling suggested that the country was sick of the shenanigans. That they wanted Brexit done, for better or worse.

Nigel said:

Losing in the stock market is easier to deal with. Finally getting rid of a long losing position is a sort of relief. It's over. You're done. You're out of it. But with winning you always feel you could have done better. That you should have gone in earlier or aimed higher. And that's what it was like with the Euro elections. *We could have done better.*

Nonetheless, we had done what we had set out to do. And maybe that's what the voters thought too because after that euphoric high, we began a long glide path back down the ratings. We were still in the game up to the general election later in the year. But the emerging truth was that the public felt the Brexit Party had served its purpose.

The first possible indication we had of that was the Peterborough by-election on 6 June.

I stayed in my office, except on the day of the by-election itself. Campaigning is best left to campaigners. Nigel was on storming form. The spirit was with him.

The stakes were high and at least some of the omens were good. The Peterborough constituency was largely Brexit-leaning (over 60 per cent voted to leave). The Labour MP had been recalled by the voters following her lying about a speeding charge and being expelled from the party. And we had an excellent local candidate.

A DIFFICULT DECISION

Other omens were less good, however. We had no history in the constituency. We had no data, no canvassing returns, no local knowledge. The election was called at short notice and so soon after the European elections that we didn't have the time or resources to focus on the seat. And Momentum claimed it mobilised nearly 1,000 activists to campaign in the area, with 500 knocking on doors to get the vote out.

Labour won by 683 votes – 2 per cent of the votes cast. Very like the margin they had won by in the 2017 general election. We came second and the Tory candidate came in 2,000 votes behind us.

Was it a fair election? We had our doubts. A Labour activist who had been convicted of election fraud was active in the campaign and was present at the count (Labour said he was there in an unofficial capacity). There were many claims of undue pressure, vote harvesting, 'bed and breakfasting[*] or maintaining a threatening presence outside the polling booths – though the police investigation ultimately concluded that no criminal activity had taken place. But the fact remained that the Labour candidate attracted just over 10,000 votes. We had achieved just under 10,000 and had split the anti-Labour vote. The successful Labour candidate said, 'the politics of division will not win', and in one unintended sense she was absolutely right. Between us and the Conservatives there were 17,000

---

[*] Taking up a temporary address in a constituency in order to vote more than once in different parts of the country.

voters who didn't want Labour – but our divided vote gave victory to Labour. It is the perennial lament of third parties.

We thought this example would have an effect as and when it came to a general election. We had shown – albeit in a way we didn't want – that our presence on the ballot paper could seriously affect an election. It truly was, as Nigel said, a 'very significant result'.

We had come from nowhere to dislodge the Tories into third place in a by-election. But we weren't resonating as a full-spectrum political party. Our name was our strength and our limitation.

So, Peterborough took some of the wind out of our sails. There was a stubborn fact that no one in the Brexit movement had ever won a parliamentary seat on their own account. Over the previous twenty years, as part of UKIP, we'd had defections of sitting councillors and we'd won both parish seats and council seats but never a parliamentary seat with an original candidate who hadn't run before. And not for lack of trying. But then, as the Brexit Party we had scooped the European elections. And if nothing else, we had prevented a Tory win in Peterborough. There was bound to be a general election soon – if it was to be a Brexit election, surely the Brexit Party would be playing a decisive role in it?

Nigel said, 'The Conservative Party are bitterly divided, and I consider it to be extremely unlikely that they will pick a leader who is able to take us out on 31 October come what may.'

A DIFFICULT DECISION

That turned out to be true: 31 October came and went and we remained members of the European Union. But there were other events before we get to that point.

Our MEPs went to Brussels. They were twenty-nine MEPs and the single largest political party in the entire European Parliament. By all accounts it had a tremendous *esprit de corps*. I was pleased to remain where I was in London. There had been talk of my taking a place on the list, but I couldn't see the need for a short spell in Brussels, no matter how interesting it might have been. Nigel's UKIP in the European Parliament was a high-energy group of people described by friend and foe alike as a 'rugby team on tour'. The team we sent in 2019 was considerably more diverse and gender-balanced but equally hilarious, and I felt there wasn't a great deal I could add.

On his return to Brussels, Nigel was immediately involved in a fracas with the European Commission. The week before the European elections, Channel 4 had run a hit piece saying that Nigel had benefited from undeclared donations from Arron Banks, of this parish. Now, the European Commission snapped into action. Two days before the Peterborough by-election – in scenes reminiscent of the Electoral Commission's investigative trip to our offices immediately before the European elections – the acting chair of the Advisory Committee on the Conduct of Members sent a letter summoning Nigel to a meeting the following day, in barely twelve hours' time. The President himself had referred the matter to the

Advisory Committee. Whichever of the EU's several Presidents it was, the highest levels of the hierarchy had turned their attentions to Nigel.

Article 5(3) and Article 4 of the Code of Conduct were cited along with Chapter 2 of its Implementing Measures. Your eyelids may be drooping at this sort of language, but for those of us who deal with these matters it was absolute catnip. If they were going to rely on Chapter 2 of the Implementing Measures, we were in the clear. That is, the charges would never stick – but then the charges weren't the point. They wanted headlines in the UK on the eve of the Peterborough by-election.

They would succeed in that. But the case is worth recording as an object lesson in how to deal with a giant, rules-based bureaucracy.

Ben Wrench, a fine legal brain, was Nigel's man in his Brussels office and I worked with Ben on the defence. The first rule is to pay close attention to every line in the charge sheet.

Luckily, before their programme was broadcast, Channel 4 had written us a letter saying the following:

> The Advisory Committee considers that Mr Farage committed a serious breach of the Code of Conduct ... [which would] merit the highest penalty foreseen by the Parliament's Rules of Procedure ... varying from a reprimand to ... the suspension or removal of the member.

They were showing off that they had access to confidential material. But as the proceedings of the committee were indeed confidential, this was prima facie evidence that Channel 4 were in receipt of stolen emails and that someone in the Brussels apparatus had stolen them.

Ben's letter to Channel 4 was a model of such letters and established subsequent cause for legal action:

> It is our view that if you make mention of this you will be in contempt of the Rules of Procedure of the European Parliament, which confirm that the proceedings of the Advisory Committee are confidential.
>
> We find it amazing that you should be in possession of this letter before Mr Farage's office in Brussels has received any such information.

This would have pleased Channel 4, but they weren't the real audience. This was aimed more at the European Commission and the rules that had been broken in Brussels.

> This demonstrates that Channel 4 is cooperating with an individual who clearly dislikes Nigel Farage but nevertheless sits on a committee which purports to make judgements about him and who by leaking this letter seeks to bounce the President into making a decision before he

has seen any evidence. This is unacceptable and a breach of protocols surrounding the operation of the committee.

Accordingly, we demand that the source of the leak is found, as clearly that person did not have an objective view of the facts and is prejudiced against Mr Farage.

It is unlikely that anyone at Channel 4 knew whether this was the case or not. The European rule book is very extensive.

We have already asked the President of the European Parliament for an investigation into the previous leak and will be repeating this request in the present circumstances.

Good work – threatening, official, legal. Did it help? They broadcast the programme and counted it a journalistic win, no doubt. It is prized in the media to reveal confidential information. And, of course, we had benefited from leaks and whistle-blowing ourselves in the past. The amazing scams operated by MEPs had all been revealed in unauthorised, confidence-breaching ways. Almost nothing ever happened, incidentally, to communitaire-minded lawbreakers.*

---

* A *Guardian* report finished with this acknowledgement of the European Commission's habitual indulgence of their parliamentary representatives: 'According to Transparency International, 24 MEPs were found to have broken ethics rules between 2014 and 2018. But only one reprimand was issued and none were sanctioned. Offences included six MEPs failing to declare luxury trips funded by Azerbaijan's autocratic government. Another MEP was censured for tabling 200 amendments to the EU's data protection rules that had been copied word-for-word from lobbyists.'

Returning to Nigel's meeting with the European Commission, I suggested that the twelve-hour notice they had given was absurd and we needed fourteen days and documents in order to proceed.

The lesson here is line-by-line resistance. Also important, make demands of your own. Ben replied to the Advisory Committee: 'Please provide us with a copy of the Rules of Procedure of your committee by 10.00 hrs tomorrow morning.'

This insinuated that their actions may have been in breach of their own rule book (a suggestion that has force in that forum).

The next step: 'Also by 10.00 hrs tomorrow morning, please confirm our understanding that all proceedings of your committee, including not only the hearing itself but also the decision to invite Mr Farage to attend, are expected to be confidential.'

This established a precondition of Nigel's appearance – it might allow for further argument and another postponement.

Ben went on to say:

> The committee, also in keeping with the rules of natural justice, will no doubt be saddened to learn that the details of the hearing and the allegations were widely leaked to the press and to Mr Farage's political opponents, even before he or his office were made aware of any investigation or the invitation to attend the committee.

It was true: before we had received the committee's letter, journalists from the BBC and the *Telegraph* had issued a long thread of tweets and an online article. The *Telegraph* quoted 'Parliament sources' to assert that 'Mr Farage is likely to be found in breach of EU rules even if he does turn up'.

This allowed us to say:

> The above breach of confidentiality is not only prejudicial to a fair hearing but also means that we can have no confidence that the hearing itself, or even this email, will remain private unless and until the parliamentary authorities have completed an inquiry into the leak and taken appropriate action to ensure it is not repeated. Accordingly, it is currently not appropriate for Mr Farage to provide you with any further information given that it may include private and commercially sensitive material that would not need to be disclosed under the Code of Conduct.

Ben concluded that the leaks to the press had breached the committee's own Rules of Procedure (note the capitals) and, perhaps mischievously, invited them to dismiss the proceedings 'in the interests of natural justice'.

The actual defence – that the money from Arron Banks was for entirely non-EU-related business, to establish a career for Nigel when his time in the European Parliament was over – would come later.

Reading the emails between Nigel's office and the European Commission, you can see that the Commission were not acting in good faith – that they were selectively leaking and that their charges had been orchestrated in an attempt to influence the polls that were opening soon.

They are, however, masters of process. If you want to mount a defence against these people and their systems, you have to play their game by their own rules.

* * *

At the risk of repeating myself, the multi-dimensional nature of politics is one of its most unacknowledged features. While great affairs of state were working themselves out above our heads, we were still concerned with the other end of the spectrum.

Our copycat provocateur, for one thing, was back in business with his website, taking £20 from one of our blameless supporters.

That supporter, Eric, unaware of what he was getting into, wrote to this individual. He said, 'Hi there: I still haven't received my membership card. Could you please let me know if there's a problem?'

He received a prompt response: 'Hi Eric: No problem, eCards will be issued by email soon. Brexit party BIP.'

Eric came back with:

I have sent the Brexit Party a couple of emails over the last few weeks asking if this was a scam. All I've heard Nigel say is that we have lots of members paying £28.00. Although I only sent £20.00, I was hoping for two membership cards, one for my wife Patricia. I am not sure what the BIP stands for so could you please explain if you are attached to Nigel Farage's Brexit Party? Regards, Eric.

Minutes later, our friend fired back:

Nigel Farage is in breach of my intellectual property The Brexit Party established 9 November 2016. He runs a passing off operation, a common law tort and we are in legal dispute with him. There is only one legitimate Brexit Party and I created it. Your membership cards will be issued in due course.

Eric responds, 'Hi. It's not your party I want to join so could you please refund my £20.00?'

I, no doubt unfairly, hear the response as a scream, perhaps in a German accent: 'I reiterate, there is only one legitimate Brexit Party and I created it on 9 November 2016. There will be no negotiation on this fact.'

Eric: 'Hi. Just to be clear, are you saying you're not refunding my £20.00?'

A DIFFICULT DECISION

I regret to say I never found out whether Eric got his money back.

And then in one packet of emails marked Legal, all relating to these weeks, there were any number of issues that required attention, some of them impossibly knowledgeable:

- It is important not to confuse a *temporary FTA* under Article XXIV (8)(b) with an *interim agreement* under Article XXIV (5)(c)... (cont. p. 64).
- A five-page opinion piece from an eminent QC was sent to us. It argued that we had already left the EU. There was much merit in his argument.
- Voter Gravity, an American company supplying us with electoral intelligence, had been denied a bank account in the UK. We needed to find an efficient way of paying their monthly fee before they stopped supplying their services.
- An excited supporter copied us into his threat of legal action against Jo Swinson for her defamatory allegations against Nigel. He wanted to know if we'd like to join the group.
- A complainant wrote saying that a Brexit activist had 'vandalised and defaced my beautiful historic property by screwing one of your Brexit Party placards to the Georgian noticeboard attached to the property'.
- The National Library of Scotland wrote asking for a copy of our European election manifesto.

- We had filmed on top of the White Cliffs of Dover and the notional owners – some trust – complained and wanted the video removed from the internet. I suggested we put them through the treatment that officials gave us and asked them to prove they owned the rights to the land via the Land Registry and that they had the legal rights to impose restrictions on filming. We dragged it out as far as was possible and eventually the complaint went away.
- The man who invented the Postie Mate (a device to protect leafleteers' fingers from dog bites) wrote to us saying that if we endorsed his product and recommended it to our leafleteers we would be protected in the event of a bitten volunteer suing us. We didn't take him up on the offer, but I feel it's worth recommending to volunteers 'before they lose a finger' as his website says (Google will locate the Postie Mate for you).
- Some quite important legal notices had gone missing because the 'forward all emails' button hadn't been toggled to 'on'. Apparently 'the system doesn't allow forwarding to addresses outside our domain without verifying the target address first'. I hadn't received something called the 'activation code email'.
- And finally, we had used the Angel of the North sculpture in Gateshead in one of our leaflets with a caption saying that after Brexit we would be able to make our own decisions about funding art (the statue, which resembles a

giant hang-glider, had been partly commissioned using EU funds). The sculptor's lawyers wrote to us with the novel legal proposition that 'Sir Antony Gormley has the right for the work not to be subjected to derogatory treatment.' It was an unlikely argument to succeed – making artists immune to criticism – but nonetheless, we had to deal with it.

* * *

While these incidents and accidents were tripping along, the Tories elected Boris Johnson as their leader and Prime Minister. A period of chaotic governance followed (who could have guessed?). We were encouraged – for all his faults, he was a Brexiteer, albeit somewhat late to the party. The colourful dramatis personae of the next three months included Boris Johnson swooping around like an out-of-control kite in the sky, the professional maniac Dominic Cummings and the Luciferian genius of John Bercow.

We had just had a rally in Birmingham with 5,000 people attending, possibly our high point. The public demand for Brexit was unabated, but Parliament steadfastly blocked any move it could, or any progress towards the end.

We felt there had to be a general election, but it was far from clear how that would come about. Nonetheless, we began to prepare for one.

Nigel called in Lesley Katon, our head of candidates, and asked her if we could find, train and field 650 candidates for a general election possibly as soon as October. It was another impossible ask, far greater than that of the European elections. She said, in a way that is characteristic of her, 'My family were market traders. We can do anything you want.'

Lesley, in a very significant way, had helped us attract support from across the political spectrum right from the start – she herself having political views leaning to the left. Her network reaches into many communities that have their roots in the Commonwealth. 'It's a complete myth that the Brexit supporters were all white British people,' she says.

> Journalists never went to speak to the Bangladesh Caterers Association, or the thousands of Chinese restaurant owners or Caribbean communities. Or British Ghanaians. Or Hong Kongers. Or Malaysians. In fact, people with roots across the globe voted to leave the EU. There was a huge amount of passionate Brexit support in these places.

And why, particularly?

> Some come from places where democracy isn't well established, or well respected. From speaking with them, it's often one of the reasons they choose to come to Britain. They tend to be conservative-minded, family-minded and

A DIFFICULT DECISION

have a strong anti-globalist strand in their thinking. And they see the EU as anti-democratic. And not very welcoming to immigrants!

There were three of us in a room once – Ann Widdecombe, Toby Vintcent and me – and we discovered we had all been involved in the Greenham Common protests. I was there shaking the wire and trying to get into the nuclear base. Ann was there with a Christian pro-Trident group, and Toby was a soldier inside the perimeter doing everything he could to keep us out. And now we were all joined at the hip in the cause of Brexit. That's a broad church.

She and Toby finished selecting the candidates by the end of August – nearly a full slate across all constituencies.

When we called for candidates, we had thousands of applications, each with a CV – often of many pages – to examine. That is a lot of reading, a lot of evaluating to do. Especially as each document had to be read by two people for independent corroboration or dispute.

How were these documents to be distributed among our evaluators? And how could we be sure that files wouldn't be left on trains or Tube seats? Leaks of candidates' names and details always had the power to ruin careers.

Toby devised a system whereby CVs were scanned and loaded onto a central database to be downloaded by members of the team. As a result, the vetting took place all over the country – it could have taken place anywhere in the world. We had people going through the documents in a car driving up the M6, in a Tuscan villa, in a cottage in Wales. The evaluations and commentaries were downloaded and uploaded in a most efficient way.

Toby and Lesley also ran the selection and maintenance of candidates. The care and control of candidates is a whole field unto itself, requiring patience, tact, diplomacy and the ability to forge enduring connections with both experienced and tyro politicians (psychologically complex and sometimes difficult sorts of people). This political fact – one of the first political facts – needs to be taken into account by anyone wanting to start a party aiming at parliamentary representation.

The candidates were vetted so successfully that almost no one got through who would embarrass the party. 'No one', as Toby says, 'who thought that homosexuality caused flooding.'

However, despite the quality of the candidates we were fielding, there was some sort of Boris effect already palpable. Voters felt he could get the thing done. We lost our prime position in the polls. Some of our candidates began to drop out.

One school of thought (not shared by myself) had it that Nigel's decision not to stand in a constituency himself caused a loss of pressure in the campaign by demoralising the troops. I completely disagreed with this – if Nigel were standing in a constituency he would be tied there. His efforts all over the country were of much more value – flying in, walking about, creating headlines wherever he landed, performing a national canvass.

And still there was deadlock in Westminster. It was all tunnel and no light.

* * *

While Nigel was battling with the European Commission and leading his new party in the European Parliament, the House of Commons was engaged in unprecedented activities quite at odds with its normal role.

Remain-minded MPs had formed themselves into an informal, ad hoc alliance and set out to influence the negotiations – and, notwithstanding the fact that such an ambition had never succeeded before, to guide them. As a token of their inexperience, they had already voted to dispense with the single most powerful weapon in the negotiator's arsenal: the ability to walk away from the table.

You don't have to be Henry Kissinger to realise this negotiating proposition is deeply flawed. If one side is not able to walk away, then that side can be bullied, pushed, manipulated into accepting things a more vigorous opponent would not countenance. And yet, parliamentarians wanted to legislate – and bind the government – to make a no-deal Brexit illegal.

To our mind, this was crazy. Or, if not crazy, it was sinister. It only made sense if you wanted no meaningful Brexit. It made sense if you wanted to maintain a subservient relationship with Brussels and rely on the European Commission's goodwill to treat the UK fairly after Brexit. We felt goodwill would be in short supply. We felt the European Commission would be more likely to want to wring our neck like a chicken's.

The unofficial Remain alliance were keeping a close eye on the goings-on in Parliament. They had heard Johnson committing to exit on 31 October 'do or die' and they guessed this meant he was preparing to leave on World Trade Organization terms, without a deal. They guessed that the Johnson administration might arrange to send Parliament home in the weeks before exit day on 31 October in order to stop MPs, with their 'meaningful vote', blocking this clean-break Brexit, and they set out to influence the business of the House and stop Johnson in his tracks.

Then there was the Benn Bill (the 'Surrender Bill') to come, and perhaps the even more extraordinary business of withdrawing the whip from twenty-one Conservative MPs who supported Oliver Letwin's 'emergency Motion' that would enable the whole omnishambles. Their sacking meant the government had no majority at all in the House, even with the support of the DUP. It was Boris Johnson's second day in Parliament and his government had no majority, a general election was impossible, and Parliament had taken over the functions of the government. No one knew what was going on. Boris was in his natural element.

The ins and outs of the time were part of a complex dance that few can rehearse or even remember.

The Speaker facilitated a Humble Address* which demanded that old messages regarding plans for a no-deal Brexit (sent by Dominic Cummings and others) be published 'not later than 11.00 p.m. Wednesday 11 September'. What a way to talk to Her Majesty – making her demand messages from Dominic Cummings!

In his last month in office, Speaker Bercow enabled the Benn Act's passage through the Commons. The so-called 'Surrender Act' dictated a letter that the Prime Minister had to send to the EU. The letter asked for a three-month extension to the Brexit deadline. Boris said he would rather be dead in a ditch than send that letter – but send it he did. (Or, to be precise, he sent two letters: the letter required by the Benn Act requesting the extension to 31 January, which Boris didn't sign, and another – which he did sign – saying he thought an extension was a mistake and asking for the EU's help in getting the country out on schedule. That started another spasm of legal activity which needn't detain us.)

The passage of the Benn Act was a *pièce de resistance*, a

---

* A parliamentary device that petitions the Queen.

grand demonstration of the supremacy of Parliament over the government. It was the Speaker's legacy, showing that the Speaker was on a level with – even superior to – the Prime Minister. He, the Speaker, could arrange matters so that the Prime Minister could be sent off to kowtow, forehead on the floor, to the European Commission.

If there is a sitcom to be written about a party start-up, there is a Whitehall farce in the events in and around the House of Commons in the year 2019.

It seemed to be clear that the only exit route was a general election. There was no other way to break the logjam. And yet, that also seemed to be impossible to achieve. The opposition parties had no appetite for a general election. Johnson tried twice in September but was defeated both times, and anyway, it would have meant Brexit would happen at the end of October with no government in power. Nor was there any majority in the House to repeal the Fixed-term Parliaments Act. There seemed to be no way out. Parliament was in a bind – it couldn't go forwards, backwards or sideways.

In an attempt to get ahead of the argument, Johnson went to the Queen to ask for Parliament to be prorogued. According to Nigel, that was 'the worst political decision ever'.

We all remember the broad outlines of what followed. Gina Miller achieved her personal best in politics by bringing a case to the Supreme Court contesting the legality of the prorogation.* She made high-minded assertions about 'subverting our democracy'. She said in *The Guardian* that the prorogation would leave 'precious little time to debate and pass any legislation to mitigate against the worst effects of a no-deal Brexit'. These were all highly political propositions and, to our way of thinking, not a matter for the courts. The former Supreme Court Justice Jonathan Sumption made the same point and Gina Miller rather grandly asserted that he had 'failed to take account of the evolutionary nature of the UK constitution'.

It was here that we looked into the make-up of the Supreme Court and found – akin to the Electoral Commission and many other parts of the Establishment – strong Remainer tendencies among its members.

And so, the Long Parliament, the Futile Parliament, the Costive Parliament resumed and the constitution, to please Gina Miller, enjoyed a burst of accelerated evolution. The Benn Act letters were sent. Brussels granted a Brexit extension beyond 31 October. Johnson failed to find a ditch to die in. There seemed to be no end to the misery.

But then a fuse blew in Jo Swinson's mind. She, the leader

---

* Ms Miller's party launch is a snapshot of how difficult it is to start a political party. Encouraged by a poll that said 66 per cent of voters would consider voting for a new party, she launched her True and Fair Party. Gilded and charismatic as she may be, and one of the leading voices of 16 million voters, she managed only thirteen attendees for her launch, most of whom were said to be her staff.

of the Liberal Democrats, came up with a remarkable proposal. There wasn't the two-thirds majority in the Commons to repeal the Fixed-term Parliaments Act but there was, with her party's cooperation along with the SNP's, a simple majority to pass the Early Parliamentary General Election Act.

It was this that broke the logjam and let the forces of democracy flow.

In the light of what ensued, Jo Swinson's decision was mysterious. Why did she decide to support a Bill that would destroy her own career? Why does any politician want an election? There's only one explanation: she thought she would win seats. Her polling – you really must beware polling – persuaded her that she would gain seats, maybe even return the party to the pre-coalition heights of sixty-two seats.

Her campaign strategy was based on revoking Article 50, something she thought to be so popular that – as she told the media – she was on course to be the next Prime Minister. A brave idea for a party with twelve MPs. The voters decided otherwise.

It turned out that we had no firm ground on which to celebrate either.

In June we were polling in the mid-twenties; in July, August and September in the mid-teens; in October we were down to 10 per cent and falling. When the election was called, we were in single figures.

However, it was still enough at that stage, we felt, to make a difference.

A DIFFICULT DECISION

* * *

Parliament was dissolved.

MPs went to their constituencies to fight for their parties and, very often, for their livelihoods. The nation breathed a vast sigh of relief. This was going to resolve, finally, for better or worse, the matter of Brexit.

We had hundreds of candidates standing all over the country. Good candidates, well kept, well looked after by Toby and Lesley. Men and women who had braved the odium of their colleagues, and even of their families in some cases.

What did we feel about our position? A realist would look bravely at the possibility that we wouldn't win any seats. But then again, based on the Peterborough result, there was a high chance we would deny the Tories seats they needed. That was the basis of our negotiation with them. We were natural collaborators. We could reach parts that Boris couldn't reach.

Ah, but the reality was – and we didn't quite realise it at the time – the Tories' animosity towards Nigel was visceral. He had been disturbing their politics for a generation. He had been viewed as a threat to their very existence. It appeared to me that this clouded their view of the opportunity now presenting itself.

In the talks I'd been having with a Tory map-maker, it was clear that they didn't understand the downside to them if they didn't agree to a non-aggression pact with us. It was a point I made to my interlocutor: 'We are taking a huge amount of Labour voters. Whoever you back cannot manage without Nigel.'

That point, soundly made at the time, appeared to be demolished by the general election result. Boris (helped by the Brexit Party's withdrawal of candidates, of course) did reach the sort of voters Nigel had mobilised previously. But in the slightly longer term, the point perhaps remains good. Boris made no lasting connection with the Red Wall voters, and the promises he made them were hollow. He banked their support and embarked on a Net Zero campaign absolutely against everything they stood for.

As a corollary to this, very many seats in the south of England and the West Country could be taken by the Liberal Democrats. The Lib Dems had been effectively wiped out in the 2015 general election, losing nearly 90 per cent of their seats. Was it fanciful to think they could rise again? Here too, the election provided a short-term judgement: Jo Swinson's fancy was a bust. She lost her own seat and the leadership of her party. But our Lazarus comparison wasn't completely dead. The Lib Dems won one of the Tories' safest seats two years later when a very large Tory majority in Chesham & Amersham went the Lib Dem candidate's way. It happened again in North Shropshire a few months later. So much of politics is the tale of unintended consequences.

A DIFFICULT DECISION

* * *

The most important factor in the election was exhaustion. After three years of fruitless negotiation and constipation in the Commons, the electorate had had enough of Brexit. More than anything else, they wanted to see it done. Any deal was better than another year of the bureaucratic to and fro.

It was when the election became inevitable that the Conservative Party machine kicked into action. It didn't turn out well for us.

One downside of a broad coalition of disparate believers rallying around one campaign flag – there isn't the (so to speak) blood connection you get between those who have fought in the trenches together for a decade. You will inevitably get those who start to believe they could effect more change by working on the inside of the Establishment. There were some of our people who assumed it would be better to switch sides from us to the Tories. They explained it to themselves perfectly well. They reasoned that their bunking off would preserve the Brexit vote at the polls.

I felt that the Conservatives could maximise a Brexit vote by giving us a clear run at a limited number of seats – possibly as few as twenty-five. Otherwise, would we repeat Peterborough, where our vote hived off half the Tory vote and let through one of our many opponents? Both sides thought so.

Initially, we thought it gave us standing in the negotiations. Our offer would be, 'Stand down a number of your candidates and give us a clear run – we will deliver seats that you can't. If you don't, we will run and neither of us will win. You will pay a terrible price.'

Their counter-offer said, 'If you stand these candidates, you will split the Brexit vote and *you* will pay a terrible price. Everything you've worked for all your political life will be lost. We won't stand down a single candidate.'

Our response to that was, 'The deal you're offering is woeful. It is very far from the clean-break Brexit we have campaigned for. The voters know it. Your "backstop" is breaking up the United Kingdom. You're giving away our fisheries. You're not even committed to deregulation.'

To that there was no response. They calculated that we wouldn't risk Brexit. They were betting we wouldn't stand against them. They were betting that they would win anyway. Their personal animosity also came into it.

It was the hardest decision that Nigel had ever had to make.

On the one hand, logic was on our side. Those Labour marginals in the Red Wall – they are culturally Brexit. The Tories had very little in common with them. It wasn't at all clear Johnson could mobilise them.

On the other hand, we all regarded another hung parliament with horror. More stagnation. More parliamentary manoeuvring. The suffocating sense of futility, of a deadlock impossible to break.

The only thing to break that deadlock might well have been a second referendum, going back to the beginning of the three-year process and starting all over again. And what if that referendum produced an even narrower margin of victory for one side or the other?

Was that what we were risking? Was our presence in the election putting Brexit in danger? Should we withdraw?

There were conversations going on at many levels between us and the Conservative hierarchy. I heard a rumour that one of our Brexit Party people was talking to senior Tories about a ministerial post in the next government.

That seemed very implausible to me. Was it true? It was true there was a rumour.

As I said earlier, when you have a cross-party group assembled for a particular purpose, there aren't the deep bonds of loyalty that can be relied on when the shooting starts. How quickly people see the advantages open to them, and how deftly they explain it to themselves as the right course, the moral course, the self-sacrificing course of action.

But such is the business we were in.

Did these semi-defections, these quasi-betrayals hurt us? It's impossible to say. Perhaps if everyone on our side had been saying the same things, behind a united front, then maybe we would have done better in the pre-election jostling for position.

The behaviour of the Conservative Party officials was easier to interpret. Several of them might have landed up in jail for corrupt practices. Offering peerages as a political inducement is a criminal offence.

My feeling was that we couldn't win any of this and that we should simply wait and see what happened.

On the instructions of Nigel, I was engaged in my own private negotiations with a close confidant of Boris. I'd rung up Nigel and ventured my thought that the position was hopeless, that the chances of winning a seat were extremely slim. My question to him was – what were the three or four main things he wanted in return for standing down candidates? He developed a list of four things we wanted, the four things that would make sense of Brexit.

The only thing we got – one thing out of four – was a guarantee we would not be bound to align our regulations with the EU.

On top of that, we were trying to get them to understand the value of an electoral pact. One message I sent said, 'We are taking a huge amount of Labour voters. Whoever you back cannot manage without Nigel. Any arrangement needs the Brexit Party to have a clear run in Labour Leave areas.'

He, and possibly others around Boris, were convinced Nigel was prepared to split the Leave vote.

Consider Nigel's position. He was Mr Brexit. In my reckoning, it had been almost entirely due to his perseverance and single-mindedness that the cause had continued for twenty years. He had enlisted many and jettisoned many. He had been buffeted, abused, betrayed. He had inspired and survived. He had invested blood and treasure in his cause for two decades. Was he now to give it all up for others to profit from? Was he to hand over all the accumulated capital from one of the most daring political ventures of his generation? Was he, by withdrawing, by standing his troops down, to pass the crown of Brexit on to a prancing Boris Johnson?

'Country before party' is an attractive slogan. It is also noble. Only when the reality is revealed is it apparent how difficult that decision is.

We had our candidates selected and ready to go. There were 200,000 supporters and 17 million Leave voters depending on what decision Nigel would take. He felt deep inside himself that a 'clean-break Brexit' was beyond Boris's abilities to achieve.

Meanwhile, the Tories were intensely active, operating on our candidates with a barrage of emails, phone calls and social media posts. Our candidates received thousands of messages after the *Daily Mail* published the email addresses of our candidates in key marginals and urged their readers to bombard them with demands they step down.

And deny it as they might, the Tories were offering

criminal inducements to our candidates. They offered Ann Widdecombe a place on the Brexit negotiation team if she would withdraw. When they denied having made such an offer, she went on television offering to swear on holy writ she was telling the truth – and we heard no more of that denial. But they were far from finished.

I received a call from George Cottrell to come over to Nigel's offices as soon as I could get there. Something had happened that was clearly illegal. Robert Rowland, a Brexit Party MEP, had delivered a message from a high-ranking Tory Party member to see if the Tories could come to an accommodation with Nigel.

'He was a wealthy, successful, well-connected man,' Nigel says. We were getting close to the moment nominations closed. Nigel recalls Rowland's words:

'I've just been with [a senior Conservative Party member]. You've won. The Conservative Party is basically the Brexit Party now.' I can't remember the exact words after that. But in return for standing down our candidates he offered us ten peerages or positions.

'And a knighthood,' I add.*

'And [chief of staff] Eddie Lister's waiting for a photograph

---

* The knighthood was clearly aimed at Nigel, who has made no secret of the fact he wishes to abolish the House of Lords.

A DIFFICULT DECISION

of you all at No. 10 on Monday.' At that point, Nigel pauses telling the story. 'So, then ... I asked my people to step outside. I didn't want anyone witnessing it. *I have never been so angry*. Their assumption that I could be bought off *nearly* made me say, "Let's go for them. Let's turn them over. Let's overturn the whole applecart." Nearly.'

George and Chris Bruni-Lowe had heard the eruption behind the closed door. They'd never heard anything like it, not before or since. I saw Nigel's face as they emerged from his office. It was very red. I had never seen it red with anger. He very rarely gets angry. Exasperated, irritated, impatient – yes. Angry, no. Basil Fawlty wouldn't last a week in politics – if you let anger get a hold of your politics, it will eat you alive.

My view was that a criminal offence had been committed and we should report it. But Nigel, at that stage, chose not to pursue it. This sort of malpractice was going on with others in the party – see, for example, Ann Widdecombe's experience. It gets reported from time to time, but, the police being what they are, very little ever comes of it. Besides, there were other, more important things bubbling in the pot.

* * *

Nigel had come to his conclusion. He – we – had been going for a final push to ensure that a proper Brexit would happen.

The Peterborough effect was the only electoral pressure we could apply.

But the Tories had calculated that we would not put Brexit in jeopardy. That Nigel would ultimately value Brexit as a greater thing than himself. That he would ultimately put country before party. And they calculated correctly.

It was clearer to them than it was to us. Nigel was troubled with the calculation: could he trust the Tories to honour Brexit? Would they come through? Or should he tour the country denouncing Johnson as a liar and declaring that the deal he was committing to was Brexit in name only?

'Ann Widdecombe saw me three days before the decision. She said, "What are you going to do?" I looked at her and said, "Ann, I don't know." She laughed and said, "I thought you'd say that."'

Could we trust these people who had disappointed us and the cause so often? The final decision was: there's no alternative. We can't do anything else.

Boris declared on Sky News that he would not permit regulatory alignment with Europe. It was the only one of our four demands he agreed to – but in some senses it was the most important.

In addition, Boris released a video in which he said, 'We can get a fantastic new free trade agreement with the EU by the end of 2020 and we will not extend the transition period.'

A DIFFICULT DECISION

We called it a very clear change of direction and Nigel said, 'It sounds a bit more like the Brexit that we voted for.'

It was enough.

A couple of days before the close of nominations, Nigel agreed to stand down 317 candidates in Conservative-held seats. We disarmed.

* * *

Standing down over 300 candidates without notice is another of the impossible things to do in politics. Three hundred and seventeen people will have made great efforts to stand and some will have made very significant sacrifices. The forces of Remain, remember, were unforgiving in their attitude towards Brexit-minded colleagues, employees, public figures. A mass cull like this would have created a furore of protest and argument. Even if 95 per cent of them agreed to follow Nigel's orders there would have been a resistance movement, possibly even of legal action. Even fifteen disappointed and determined candidates can make an awful mess of a political decision.

A clever manoeuvre here got the thing done. Some will consider it a dirty trick; others will applaud it for its ingenuity and efficiency. I fall back on the idea that, in words we have seen before in this little book, politics is a rough old game.

In short, days before the close of nominations, Paul Oakden,

Nigel's chief of staff, changed the party's nominating officer. This is the official responsible for issuing the candidates' papers, processing them and lodging them with the authorities. When the nominating officer was changed, all nomination papers became invalid – the wrong signature was on the nomination form. Only the candidates we wanted to stand were reissued with the correct papers and only they were entitled to stand.

There was pushback, understandably so, and sometimes furiously so. There were demands for recompense for time and expenses incurred. Some candidates felt more strongly than others and some were understandably bitter.

We had participated in an electoral pact. There was a consequence flowing from the move that may have contributed to the election result. The voting public do not like collusion between parties.

Lynton Crosby's instructions to Johnson to concentrate on the slogan Get Brexit Done meant the voting public transferred all their Brexit energies and sympathies from us to the Tories. We went to 2 per cent.

We had been, as politicians always are in a healthy democracy, schooled by the electorate.

* * *

Should we have stood everyone down? Should we have said, 'Our work is done. We have managed to do what we set out to do. We're going to leave it to the established Conservatives to finish it off'?

Such an ending might have had more clarity; it certainly would have been neater. It would also have resulted in another twenty-five seats for the Tories.[*] But it was too late. The momentum behind us was too strong. So many candidates, so many supporters. We couldn't pack up our tents entirely. Nor did we truly believe that the Tories would finish the work as we wanted it. We felt they would never be able to deliver a clean break. Their determination would be eaten away, their negotiators would fail. We predicted there'd be a hard border in Northern Ireland. The fisheries would be given away. We had no confidence they and the civil service would deregulate. The experience of the last couple of years has shown those fears to be well-founded. The notionally Conservative, Brexit-minded government has done nothing to deregulate, open up, release.

Had the Brexit Party still been carrying the flame, would that have secured a proper exit?

Who knows?

The fact was that the party had been a brilliant campaign to deliver one outcome. The aftermath was for a different body, a different sensibility, different skill sets.

And besides, the party leaders had a different conclusion

---

[*] According to *The British General Election of 2019* by Robert Ford, Tim Bale, Will Jennings and Paula Surridge (Macmillan, 2021).

in mind. The Brexit Party was going to be renamed, retooled and sent back into the world as Reform UK, led by Richard Tice.

But that's another story altogether.

CHAPTER TEN

THE FUTURE OF POLITICAL START-UPS

What does all this suggest to us?

History tells us that parties in the UK are resilient. They refuse to die. They wax and then wane and then waste away. And just when they're ready to be buried they come dancing from their unfilled graves and swarm the House of Commons (see the Lib Dems in 2010 – and possibly again at the next general election).

Labour carries the values of the left. The Conservatives are perceived to represent the right. And the Liberals – or the Liberal Democrats – are the repository of educated individuals disaffected with the other two parties. Sometimes they lean Liberal, sometimes they lean Social Democrat, sometimes they lean Marxist, depending on where they are standing and to whom they are talking.

The Lib Dems, let it be said, have the merit of forty years of organising in constituencies. They are known to be assiduous. And other epithets I won't repeat. They have been a long-term presence knocking on doors, leafleting, foot-slogging.

You'd think there ought to be an equivalent party on the right, taking, on election night, between 5 and 25 per cent of the vote. And yet there's no sign of such a thing.

Many want it, many assume it must happen, because the political gap is wide and politics abhors a vacuum. So many people are politically homeless, disillusioned and unable to find a party which represents their hopes and aspirations. But creating a party is much more difficult than it seems (as we have seen here).

And then there is the door-to-door nature of politics. The local councillor nature of politics. The getting elected to school boards. The years of farming a constituency before harvesting it.

The sense that a banner hoisted for 'common sense' is ever going to become a parliamentary presence is, probably, a delusion. The Enough Is Enough Party is never going to get an elected representative under our electoral system.

Even when parties lose their way like Labour in the 1980s and the Tories in the 1970s (and, indeed, now) they can be resurrected by some genius finding and redefining their ancestral purpose. The 'property-owning democracy' of Mrs

Thatcher. The 'traditional values in a modern setting' of Tony Blair's Labour. Each of those titans found the meeting point between their party and the great, mildly aspirational, small-c conservative majority that is middle England.

I have said to Nigel I thought he was not a politician (in that he did not have the dishonesty of a politician). Rather, he was much more of a campaigner. He thought about that for a moment or two and agreed – albeit in a way that left his options open.

Brexit was a brilliant, twenty-year campaign. A single issue with a single objective. And it succeeded without a single MP elected solely in its cause.

What that experience suggests to me is this. If you want something specific changed in the body politic, you will not get elected on a single-issue platform under our voting system. Not rejoining the EU. Not on an anti-climate change platform, nor Reform the NHS, nor Bring Common Sense Into Teaching. Quite apart from the difficulties of starting a political party, under first past the post you will not get your candidates into Parliament.

So, if we want to have legislative influence, how do we do that?

We have to learn from the left – they who have swept all before them over the past twenty-five years. They understood, long before we on the centre-right did, that culture is upstream of politics.* People who aren't interested in politics are shaped by culture. Our opponents achieved their ends, almost without our being aware of it. The centre ground has been pulled to the left by two or three generations of long marchers who started out in the teacher training colleges and are now inheriting the West. Received opinion in our schools, universities, cultural and administrative institutions – as well as in big boardrooms – is all of the progressive left. Their victory is so complete that they have altered the language in such a way that it will become impossible to think certain thoughts because there won't be the language for it (George Orwell was right).

This is no place to go into the inventory of the values and attitudes of the progressives.

If we want to counter the left – or even if you want to counter them – there's little joy in starting a party that stands candidates in constituencies. Everything in this book supports that proposition. Creating a party is too difficult. The compliance is too hard to comply with. The environment you put yourself into is unremittingly hostile. The personalities are too chaotic. The system is against you. And even if you get a few MPs, you are still nowhere near your objective.

Apart from the phenomenal difficulties of getting someone elected, the successful MP will have no influence on the

---

* Andrew Breitbart's doctrine.

legislative process; he or she will be lonely and alone. So, don't try to disrupt the two- or three-party system. It takes too long. And for the same reason, don't try to change the voting system. Not only does it take too long, the voting public just isn't interested.

So, what is the way forward? Earlier in this book we noted the thing that persuaded Theresa May to leave office. It was the message from her backbenchers that *they would lose their seats* if she went on. That is the pressure point a political movement seeks to operate on.

An MP is a vulnerable person. Most have no other source of income. In the event of losing a seat, there is a payment which looks generous but largely goes on the expense of closing their offices. Jobs for ex-MPs are not as common as people think. Losing a seat is a momentous personal event for an MP. And therein lies the way of new-party, no-party politics.

It is a way that has an immediate effect: it works now, before the next election. A way of acting that will change the priorities of sitting MPs. And that is done by making them aware of opinion in their electorate. It projects the idea into a sitting MP's head that there is a community in their constituency that will vote against them at the next election. Their re-election is under threat, their seat, their livelihood. The sitting MP understands that an organised body of opinion can – within their own party – get officers onto the selection committee with the ultimate and immediate humiliation of deselection.

Entryism is a powerful threat because it can be brutally effective. The precise details of how to organise a local campaign to turn the constituency party to your purposes depends entirely on the party's rule book. This is obtainable from the association office. You will need to study it carefully, in the knowledge that your opponents know it intimately. Your strategy will depend entirely on what you find written there. Maybe it is best to get your people elected to the selection committee. Maybe it is best to call a special general meeting where a vote of no confidence in the sitting MP can be called. Maybe the mere threat of such measures will persuade the MP to incline in your direction. Maybe that sense of a large, organised body of opinion among the MP's electors will persuade him or her of their perilous position.

For all my scepticism about it, this idea relies heavily on social media. Exactly how this marshalling of opinion will work, I leave to others skilled in the art of it.

In the early phase, the operation might look more like a news magazine, or a social media site. It might be producing messages and stories in visual form with pictures and headlines, content that is amusing, startling, challenging, interesting. It might comment daily on what the media is telling us. It would be political but appeal more as a cultural vehicle.

Far from being a traditional party, this movement needn't even have a name in the first instance. It would articulate and project the values that define a certain cast of mind, a certain sort of voter.

The operation will need some essentials:

- Funding, and in quite reasonable amounts. Not the many millions needed for running representatives, but (I pull a figure out of the air) a million a year for five or ten years.
- An office with a general manager, a social media editor, a website genius, a number of writers (some with a humorous bent), a creative director with graphic design skills (Extinction Rebellion has clearly acquired the services of a brilliant creative director). A finance officer will be essential, perhaps performing company secretary duties in terms of GDPR compliance. In all, perhaps a dozen people crammed into an office, bouncing ideas off each other and firing out material every day to amuse and move the spirit of people who might be encouraged in as supporters at a later date. The office would identify and commission campaigns to engage in actions alongside like-minded organisations.
- And externally, 500 keyboard warriors who can share the memes, tweets and messages to their various audiences. The operation might have travelling comedians who can

be deployed to subvert demonstrations and die-ins with humour and satire. Extinction Rebellion's Red Rebel Brigade couldn't withstand much comical commentary delivered through a loudspeaker.

The purpose of the project is to produce a microcosm of a broad-based British culture. The features of this culture are an easy acceptance of the eccentricities of human life while retaining a solid grasp of the pleasant British values of friendliness, neighbourliness and that appetite for comic observation you find in good conversation. It's about a way of getting on with each other – very different individuals as we may be – without getting angry. It's the art of seeing and listening to the other side of the argument. It's the way of facing up to one another and looking for common ground rather than searching out reasons to dislike each other.

Unless a full-spectrum party proceeds from a culture – not from an idea or from a single issue – it won't succeed. Where the leader, the voice, the person in whom this culture vibrates – where he or she comes in – that remains to be seen. There is still an obvious candidate in Nigel Farage – but politics is the most unpredictable of human occupations.

CONCLUSION

So was it, after all, worthwhile? Was it worth all the expense, the time, the energy?

It was a year such as none of us had experienced before – it's very unlikely any of us will again. We did the impossible thing – we magicked up a political party in a matter of months, campaigned for our candidates, won.

We became the largest party in the European Parliament. We confirmed to the world that the UK still had an appetite for Brexit. We gave history a good bit of a shove in our direction.

Nigel Farage hit the highest point of his 25-year political career and (with the media career that followed) established himself as a permanent part of British political discourse.

But then again, we never solved the mystery of how to establish a popular, well-supported, full-spectrum party. Once the public saw our single issue had been resolved, they transferred their support to the party they saw as delivering the practical results.

Was their faith justified? Or did we achieve freedom in name only?

When Nigel wrote a piece in the *Daily Mail* saying how pleased he was that Brexit had been delivered, I was somewhat upset. In my view, Johnson had only delivered Theresa May's deal minus the obligation for regulatory alignment. Yes, that was a key element of our sovereign freedom – but only if you actually pursue deregulation. In the years since our Independence Day there has been very little evidence of that. Did the 'Brexit Freedoms Bill' as set out in the Queen's Speech come to anything? It befuddles me that a party with an eighty-seat majority has so massively failed to make any real progress towards a Brexit dividend.

How we can still be subject to the jurisdiction of the European Court of Justice makes one despair. Three years after Brexit we still don't control our borders, and we have failed to separate ourselves from the European Court of Human Rights (essential, if we are to control our borders). The burden of regulation is probably slightly more burdensome than it was. The civil service, with their heavy Remain bias, seems impervious to the wishes of their political masters – let alone to the wishes of the voting public.

It has become clear that Johnson never understood the

CONCLUSION

downsides of his rehashed Theresa May deal; he only understood the need to get elected. He believed that having signed a treaty, he could renegotiate – or even resile from – it at his leisure.

There never was an oven-ready deal. Perhaps we should have been more aware of what everyone else seemed to know instinctively: Boris Johnson is not a reliable ally. Worse than that – he is a campaigner, not a Prime Minister.

As a result, the Brexit bonus has never arrived. The 2022 Queen's Speech offered the bonfire of the EU's vanities – the GDPR, directives, quangos, the whole apparatus of Continental dirigisme. But they are finding it an impossibly lengthy process to repeal redundant EU legislation. Why it should be so, none of us understand. The civil service say it's impossible. It's too difficult. It's too time-consuming. But then, they are also refusing even to come into the office. They are civil servants – government employees who left people to die outside the airport during the evacuation of Afghanistan because their shift was over. Repealing EU regulations features very far down their list of priorities.

Alas, the trade deals are less significant than their promoters claim (also negotiated by Remainer civil servants). Our farmers will struggle to compete with Australian beef and wheat and New Zealand lamb. Our fisheries still suffer – that beggars belief. Add to that, the consequences of the Windsor Framework have yet to play out fully – there might yet be some very alarming consequences falling out of that terrible concession to the EU's punitive negotiation stance.

When I was talking to my third party, who had Boris's ear at the time, all these issues were made known to him. It cannot be said that Covid is the reason for the delay in bringing about the Brexit bonus. In short, Johnson did not achieve Brexit as he claimed he would, leaving the British public disillusioned. But Brexit was never going to be achieved as it should have when the money due to the EU was paid before a deal had even been reached.

Furthermore, Nigel was pushed into the long grass by Johnson and his associates, meaning an opportunity to create a trade deal with the US was lost – Donald Trump having first opened the door to the idea that Nigel could have an ambassadorial relationship with the US, helping to negotiate a mutually beneficial post-Brexit trade deal. This lost opportunity is demonstrated by Rishi Sunak's abject failure to strike up a trade deal with President Biden. It seems the Prime Minister is just as effective at negotiating trade deals as he is at stemming the tide of illegal immigration.

I can only hope that, faced with the looming recession, raw material shortages and rising inflation, we start to take seriously the idea that EU regulation is a great and unnecessary constraint on economic growth.

So, the jury's out on whether it was worthwhile. Even with

the government's whopping majority, opportunities are being abandoned, week by week, month by month.

It's often said that political careers end in failure. We see that all the time, and some of us feel it in our bones. There is another saying that may or may not be true, but it helps us all keep going, each in our own way. It says, 'Everything will be all right in the end. And if it isn't all right, it isn't the end.'